THE RABBIT'S LAID AN EGG, MISS!

Life as a London Headteacher

Mike Kent

Trentham Books

Stoke on Trent, UK and Sterling, USA

Trentham Books Limited
Westview House   22883 Quicksilver Drive
734 London Road   Sterling
Oakhill   VA 20166-2012
Stoke on Trent   USA
Staffordshire
England ST4 5NP

First published 2006

British Library Cataloguing-in-Publication Data
A catalogue record for this book is available
from the British Library

ISBN 10-digit: 1 85856 406 9
ISBN 13-digit: 978 1 85856 406 7

Cover illustration: Paul Bommer

Designed and typeset by Trentham Print Design Ltd,
Chester and printed in Great Britain by Cromwell
Press Ltd, Trowbridge

CONTENTS

The joy of Mike Kent's columns

There were two points of sanity and humour in this crazy world of education, Ted Wragg and yourself. Now, for the moment, there's only one. Martin Dove, *TES* reader

I always enjoy illustrating Mike's columns. They are witty, informed and filled with common sense. Paul Bommer, illustrator

Mike's school is an exceptionally popular and happy one. His writing shows why. Gerry Blinston, Assistant Director, Achievement: Southwark Education Authority

Whenever I read Mike's column, I feel there is some sanity left in education. Peter Gordon, *TES* reader

I opened my TES *this morning, read your article, and fell out of bed laughing.* Sandra Shepherd, *TES* reader

Our supply teachers love going to Mike's school, and when you read his TES *column, you understand why they have such a good time.* Fiona Leloup, Director, Classroom Supply Teacher agency.

I passed your article to several colleagues... and every one of them nodded vigorously in agreement. Andrew Clarke, *TES* reader

In his hugely enjoyable columns, Mike charts the good, bad and downright loony things teachers and schools contend with these days. Now they're in a book, and we can enjoy them all again. Beryl Pooley, retired Headteacher

Your article on school inspections was brilliant... no two ways about it. John Gooseman, *TES* reader

I always look forward to your column on Fridays. It is witty, relevant, and always great fun to read. Ron Morgan, *TES* reader

Your humorous writing is always rooted in common sense and human values. Alan Barton, *TES* reader

Your column in the TES *is always the first thing I read.* Andrea Reading, *TES* reader

Your column this week made me realise once again how lucky our readers are to have someone so positive and upbeat. Bob Doe, previous Editor, *TES*

Foreword

Surprisingly, Mike Kent was a 'reluctant' columnist for the *Times Educational Supplement*. Over the years he'd written occasional features for us and I got to know him through long telephone conversations. He'd tell me stories of life in Comber Grove primary which would end with both of us in giggles.

Late in 2000, *FRIDAY magazine* – a weekly publication within the *TES* – was on the lookout for a new contributor. Mike was our first choice. All those tales of school life. But no, he wasn't interested. Didn't have time, he said. Comber Grove and its pupils took up every hour. That sums Mike up. He is always there for the children, staff and parents. They come first.

Then three weeks later came a call that lifted my spirits. 'I think I can do it.'

And he's been doing it for the past six years. From his first column in early January 2001 he's made *TES* journalists and readers laugh – and sometimes reflect. He's talked about school plays, guitar lessons, assemblies, parents, unwise government diktats ... and my favourite: faltering first love by the water fountains.

I know it's all true. I became a governor at Comber Grove five years ago and spend many hours in the school. I've watched it as it happens!

Read this collection and enjoy the columns as much as our readers have. I know, because they tell me.

Jill Craven
Deputy editor, *Friday magazine*
The Times Educational Supplement

Dedication

For Jill, who started all this

Introduction

I think I'd always wanted to be a teacher.

Even as a young child, I'd set up the blackboard and easel my dad had made for me, and play schools with the neighbours' children during the holidays. I'd set them little tasks, and then have individual talks with them about their work in the garden shed, mentally converted into the teacher's office. I don't even think they complained when I told them off.

Getting into training college wasn't too difficult, either. I chose the one beginning with 'A' at the top of the list, and told my headmaster I was applying. Since he was on first name terms with the college principal, I was given a place that September.

I started my career in Islington in the sixties, during the heady days following the Plowden Report. It was a report that completely changed the face of primary education. Children no longer sat in rows, all doing the same thing at the same time. Variety was the order of the day, children were encouraged to work at their own pace, and up to six different activities could be going on at the same time. If it was done well, a primary classroom was an exciting place, and I revelled in the freedom to structure my day as I wanted.

But with so many things going on simultaneously, ensuring that every child was making adequate progress became a delicate balancing act, and lots of teachers struggled to make the best of a fully integrated day. Children in the inner cities – often not surrounded at home by books, good conversation, music and creative activity – tended to suffer most. They needed much more structure in the classroom, often didn't get it, and many moved to secondary school unable to cope with basic English and maths. Nevertheless, I was always proud that children who'd been through my classroom could not only read, write, and add up well, they'd also had a thoroughly enjoyable time too.

I moved on to deputy headship... and then headship at the start of the eighties, coinciding with the newly elected Conservative government. Huge changes again: a national curriculum for primary schools so complex it was impossible to cram it all into the school year. It was hurriedly changed... and then changed again. Before long, each time a new version emerged the previous version was put into our school museum, even though it had only been around for a few months. The amount of money wasted was truly staggering.

You'd have thought that lessons would have been learned. But no, we're well into the 21st century, where young children are tested every five minutes, initiatives like the 'literacy hour' come, fail and go, teachers have to write a risk assessment if they as much as light a candle, and schools now have to cope with a constant barrage of initiatives, competing with each other and looking over their shoulders in case a team of inspectors is heading in their direction to tell them they're falling apart.

And yet... I'm still here, because children are children, schools can be fascinating and enjoyable places and it doesn't have to be like that. We all need to pop our heads over the parapet occasionally.

I think I've been very lucky with my choice of career. There has never been a day when I've woken up and thought 'I really don't feel like going to work today'. The primary school environment can be so rich, so full of amusing incidents, that each week can hold an abundance of treasures.

I hope this book will demonstrate that.

MIKE KENT

1

God, another hour before playtime...

I was a bit wary about becoming the head of a primary school. As a junior teacher, I'd rarely encountered a child under seven, and infant teachers never ventured into the junior part of the building. That's how it was. We kept ourselves to ourselves.

Then, suddenly, I had to acknowledge the existence of very small children and know about their curriculum. I soon found that reading stories or doing science experiments with them is extremely pleasurable, with the added bonus – for a head – of not having to teach them all day. Until Miss Smith, in Reception class 1, is away.

You stare at the message in disbelief. Miss Smith is never ill. That's one of the reasons you put her in Reception class 1. Your supply agencies are suffering the flu season, and they've already sent their remaining Australians to every school except yours. Your part-timers aren't available either. You realise you'll be teaching Class 1 yourself, and you hurry to the staffroom for the keys.

They're not on the hook. You grab an older child from the playground and tell him to find the premises officer for the spare set. Then you hunt for the register and money tin, and go to meet your charges like a shell-shocked soldier.

They're lined up, eager, and they look at you with interest. So do their mothers. 'You'll have to be good today,' says one to her tiny daughter. 'You've got Mr Kent.' It's a friendly Monday morning joke, but the child bursts into tears.

I get the children through the door and they hang their coats up. Thomas shrieks. While trying to get his coat over his head, his zipper has jammed. I release his head, comfort him, the door is opened, and somehow we all reach the carpet.

Monday dinner money is a nightmare. It's combined with money for film club, biscuits, books, raffle tickets. Sensible parents – how I love them – have put it all in an envelope, labelled appropriately. Other children clutch several coins and haven't a clue how much they've got, or what it's for. Andrew has 2p and tells me it's for everything. The door opens and Samantha's mum appears, with Samantha in tow. Sorry they're late, but they had a bit of trouble, and how much does she owe from three weeks ago?

I abandon the register and make a list of who's paid what, dispatching it upstairs in the care of two children I consider reliable. Moments later, I hear the tin clatter down the stairs. Javed says: 'Miss never sends Alan. He drops things.'

The children are fidgeting on the carpet now and one of them breaks wind loudly. I wonder how on earth Miss Smith manages to do her Monday money-gathering so efficiently. It's a skill I've never fully appreciated.

I decide to read a story. I'm good at that, and it will occupy us for a while. I select a book and Troy raises his leg, shouting my name urgently. I look at him in panic. 'I've got new shoes on, Miss,' he says, gender recognition not featuring largely in his life so far. Then Simone pipes up:

'You know what? Not this Saturday or next Saturday but the next Saturday after that, it's my birthday.' I tell her I'm pleased, but just now we're having a story. 'I've heard that one,' says Omari. Well, that's nice, I suggest, but possibly others in the class haven't. 'Yes we have,' they chorus. I select another. 'We've had that one too,' Omari says.

'I've got a good idea,' I say brightly, hunting for something within their experience, 'We'll draw pictures of Miss Smith, and we'll each think of something we can write about her.' The idea appeals and they settle in their seats. Fifteen seconds later they've finished their pictures. I look at the clock. Dear God, another hour before we even hit playtime.

Suddenly, the door opens and the secretary brings in someone I've never seen before. 'A supply teacher,' she says. 'The new agency had one.' I'm so relieved I resist the temptation to throw my arms around her and give her a kiss. In a moment she's gathered the children, taken artefacts from her bag and launched into a lesson. When I return in half an hour, the class is happy and attentive.

Perhaps the current obsession with targets, performance management, and thresholds puts us in danger of forgetting the skills of young teachers like Miss Smith, who, thank heavens, can cope with the form-filling but still see the real wood for the trees.

2

As usual, it all started innocently enough

Mejrid and Cerice are in the same maths group, and Cerice, kind soul, lent Mejrid her calculator. Impressed, Mejrid lent her his colouring pencils. Things moved rapidly, and soon Mejrid was passing notes expressing his affection and spending much of his dinner hour chasing Cerice around the playground.

Then, finding himself financially embarrassed on the day of our St Valentine's cake sale, he persuaded me to lend him 25p so that he could buy her a little cake with a heart on top. So far, so innocent. Being in love is one of life's pleasures, Spring was in the air, and as usual, it had all started innocently enough.

Other Year 6 boys, impressed by Mejrid's infatuation, also began directing their attention to the girls. Unfortunately, their approach was less refined. Huddling in packs by the boiler house wall like teenage boys at their first dance, they suddenly swarmed towards the girls, their hands raised as they pretended to smack them across the bottom. The girls squealed and ran away until, breathless and giggling, they regrouped by the water fountain and then made faces at the boys, whereupon the whole cycle started again.

Next morning Mrs Brown asked to see me. She was very concerned about the inappropriate sexual behaviour her daughter was experiencing, and that wasn't what she sent her to school for. Several boys, and Beyjou in particular, had been cavorting around the girls in a disgracefully sexual manner and her daughter had been extremely distressed by it. She hadn't even been able to eat her TV dinner.

I was taken aback, since Andrea had been prominent in the goading of the boys, but I listened politely, pointing out that I always spent the last 15 minutes of the lunch hour in the junior playground, and that I hadn't seen anything that had given me cause for concern. I also remembered that Andrea was extremely skilled at winding her mother up. It wasn't the first time Mrs Brown had stormed into school.

'I've told Andrea to let me know if Beyjou comes anywhere near her today,' she concluded. 'And if he does, I'll fucking kill 'im.'

Later that morning, a delegation of three mothers appeared, demanding that I do something or they would go to the police. 'Do something about what?' I asked. 'Sex games,' said Mrs Stern. 'Mrs Brown says they're rubbing themselves up against each other. My husband is disgusted.' The others nodded. Presumably their husbands were wallowing in disgust, too. When they'd gone, I warned the lunchtime helpers to keep a very close watch.

Early Thursday morning, at whistle time, I glanced out of my window. Mrs Stern was berating a crowd of older boys, wagging her finger at them. Then she stalked across the playground and shouted at Beyjou's father, who was standing quietly with his son waiting for the whistle. Other parents became animated, and the teacher on duty motioned Mrs Stern towards my room. I sighed inwardly as she hurtled along the corridor.

'I wasn't making any trouble,' she protested. 'I was just telling the boys to keep away from our girls. I told them if they want a bum to slap they can come and slap mine, and see where that gets them...'

By 9.30 I had the whole of Year 6 in the hall, pointing out that new, inoffensive games had to be found, or my hair would drop out from the stress of it all. At !0 o'clock, Mrs Brown was back in my room.

'I know what it is,' she said triumphantly. 'It's because they've started swimming on Tuesday mornings. They see each other's lumps and bumps. You'll have to take swimming off the curriculum...'

Frankly, it's not the children who are a concern. It's their parents we need to worry about.

3

So how did Mrs Green get her Jimmy in here, then?

Parents instinctively know what they want from primary education for their children, and they'll soon find which schools in an area are worth attending. A parent new to the area will simply chat to her neighbours, and assemble a shortlist, usually a very short one indeed. And since the Government has said parents have the right to send their offspring to any school of their choice, off they go to the one they've chosen. Which will be full. The head will then have to explain the 'admission criteria', and the more he or she tries to explain it, the less the parent understands. Kafka is a doddle in comparison.

'But I only live two streets away,' Mrs Jones says. 'That's true,' I reply, 'but everybody we've admitted into that year group lives nearer.'

'Well, how is it that Mrs Smith has got her children in here then?' Mrs Jones persists. 'She lives further away than me.'

'Because Mrs Smith's children are in a different year group, and there were spaces.' Mrs Jones begins to get a little irritated. 'Well, what about Mrs Brown, then? Her kids come from East Dulwich and that's miles away.'

I sigh; I've been over this ground so often. 'Mrs Brown originally lived just over the road,' I explain. 'She's been rehoused in East Dulwich but her children are still entitled to come here.'

'Then how did Mrs Green get her Jimmy in here? She lives in the same flats as me.'

'True. But Jimmy lives one floor lower than you.'

'So what?'

'It makes Jimmy 10 yards nearer. And we have to measure it all out on a large-scale map. Look, I'll show you. You can check it yourself if you like.' The conversation continues in this vein for twenty minutes and I always end up explaining the classic Catch-22 situation about the first admission rule, which is that other members of the family can come in if one of them is already attending. The trouble is, of course, you've got to get one on roll in the first place, which brings everything back to distance again.

It's all very confusing for parents, but they do have one potent weapon. The admission appeal. Providing they can make a really good case for getting a child into the school they've chosen, there's a good chance they'll win, and the school is then obliged to take the child over and above the legally specified intake number. Some parents even employ lawyers.

If there are lots of appeals, and half a dozen are successful, the school can have a real problem. These days, more and more parents are opting for this route, some of them becoming increasingly wily in the methods they use to gain entry.

Appeals are heard by a group of independent panel members, with the parent and school putting their respective cases. The appeal committees aren't daft, of course, and they can usually spot a forged doctor's letter or a dodgy rentbook.

But a while back I seemed to be at the mercy of two regular panel members who believed everything the parents said, and nothing I said. My Reception class numbers were growing alarmingly, it was becoming had to teach the children effectively, and appeals were being heard virtually every week. I even took photographs along to the appeals, to show how crowded the classrooms were, but it made no difference. Then a parent won an appeal after saying she lived very close to our school, when in fact there were four others nearer to her. I needed to find a solution, and after a hasty meeting with my staff we came up with a cunning plan.

I wrote to both panel members, inviting them into school to see the effect the overcrowding was having. They dutifully arrived and I opened the door to one of the Reception classrooms. They were horrified; children were crammed into every nook and cranny, virtually standing on each other's shoulders, while the harassed teacher rushed around.

We moved through all the infant classrooms; they saw an identical scene in each. Both left the site subdued and concerned. Once they'd gone, we quickly returned to normality, and the 13 extra children we'd been shipping from classroom to classroom just ahead of the visitors went back to their normal classes.

It seemed to do the trick. In subsequent appeal sessions, the panel members gave parents' cases a great deal more scrutiny. And the education we could offer our Reception children returned to its previous high standard.

4

From the start, Lorraine's talents were remarkable

Teaching assistants sometimes don't seem to have much going for them. They're paid very little, they supervise playgrounds in bitter weather, the children often give them only grudging respect, and yet they'll be the ones who sit in emergency departments with sick children for hours while the school attempts to contact a parent on a mobile that's usually switched off.

Certainly the job has changed over the years, and it's more interesting now. Years ago, when I was a class teacher, my school had three 'helpers' who dispensed milk, washed paintpots, brewed tea for teachers on playground duty, or tried to control classes during rainy playtimes while teachers went off for a quick ciggy. Nobody had explored the notion that they could be of real value in the classroom. Nowadays, helpers are 'Teaching assistants', vital cogs in the educational wheel and enjoying as much work variety as the average teacher. If there's going to be a fight, or if Year 5 gangs up on Year 6 after the usual rule-free chaotic football game, it's the TA's who sort it out, because by the time a teacher gets there, it's usually too late. Which brings me to Lorraine.

Lorraine was the kind of TA you want them all to be. I remember the day she came in, looking for a place for her son. We were full and, though he was an exceptionally pleasant boy, I had to turn them away. Then, before they'd left the building, one of my teachers mentioned that she'd just passed a woman in the bottom corridor who was saying to her son how attractive the school seemed, and what a shame it was that there were no places. I sent a child downstairs to find them, and Lee had a place the next day. Soon, Lorraine joined us too, working full time as a TA.

From the start, her talents were remarkable. Her warm personality and delightful humour ensured she related well to everyone. Children, especially those with special needs, made rapid progress with her, and she'd spend hours at home preparing interesting things for them to do. Perhaps because she'd been through a disastrous relationship herself, she had great empathy with children who were going through family crises that affected them deeply. Fights and major arguments in the playground dwindled; she had the knack of dissolving tension with well-aimed humour and the talents of a skilful judge and jury. She was artistic, too, and a meticulous model-maker, demonstrating in assembly how she created Victorian doll's houses that could have sold in the finest toy shops. Her talents extended in every direction. Need a complex costume for the school play or a work display completed because the inspectors are visiting? No problem. Ask Lorraine.

We thought the world of her. And then, shortly after her 38th birthday, we found out she had cancer. She'd had stomach trouble for some time, and been prescribed various pills and potions, but ultimately a scan revealed the worst.

Determined to overcome this latest difficulty in her life – after all, she'd overcome the others – she tackled chemotherapy with a grim determination and, apart from her hospital sessions, she was seldom away from the job she loved. Support from colleagues was abundant. She struggled on, determined that her friends, colleagues and children at the school should never know how ill she really was. I remember coming down a staircase and finding her in tears at the bottom. She'd just returned from the hospital. I stopped on the stairs, took hold of her, and hugged her tightly. I felt totally helpless.

A month later she was dead. This gentle, kind and unbelievably brave woman had given 10 years of dedicated service to us and been much loved for it. The funeral was some distance away, and I took the unprecedented step of closing the school so that all of us could attend. Just two parents objected – one saying it would be inconvenient to keep her child at home that day and the fact that somebody had died 'really wasn't her problem'.

Lorraines may be few and far between, but there are plenty of Teaching Assistants doing a brilliant job every day, often with little thanks. Perhaps you ought to find the nearest one in your school now... and give her a hug.

5

'Sir,' said Jason, 'Some bloke's just given me this'

I haven't put a notice in the middle of my playground saying 'No parents past this point', but just occasionally I feel like it.

Don't get me wrong; most parents are supportive and value the school highly, like Siobhan's mum who runs a cafe and won't let truck drivers have their tea and two slices until they've bought five tickets for the Christmas raffle. Nevertheless, few weeks pass without an incident with a parent, and some are bizarre enough to be unbelievable to people who don't work in a school. Take last Monday, for instance.

The first port of call in a school is the secretary, and mine has a temperament serene enough to calm a tornado. Amidst the chaos of the dinner registers, parents wanting to buy school jumpers and the repairman dismantling the photocopier, a mother strode through the queue and demanded to know why her child had been refused a place in the reception class. The secretary led her to one side and patiently explained how we had to follow the local education authority's admission criteria, that there were three admission rules, that we were only allowed to put 45 children into the year group, that we had to measure distances and admit those living nearest, and that, if she was dissatisfied with our decision, she could appeal to the authority. The mother pulled herself up to her full height and looked angrily at my secretary.

'That's all very well,' she said fiercely. 'But I want to know why I can't get my boy into this school.'

One parent did get his child into the school, but in a most unusual way. A young father appeared in our doorway just before lunch with a baby in his arms, saying he wanted to register a child and he'd like her to start today. I asked how old the child was and which school she currently attended. He nodded at the baby he was carrying. 'It's this one,' he said.

I took a deep breath and explained that educating children several months old wasn't within our brief, and although he could apply for a nursery place, she wouldn't be eligible until she was three. 'That's no good,' he said. 'My wife's left me and I've got to go to work.' Astonished, I explained that we didn't have child-minding facilities and he'd need to look for help elsewhere. Grumbling loudly, he hurried down the corridor, and I went off to have lunch with the children.

Five minutes later, Jason from Year 6 appeared from the playground and came to my table with the baby in his arms. 'Sir,' he said unhappily, 'a bloke's just given me this.' My stomach sank. I hurried outside to catch the father, but he'd gone. A teaching assistant took the baby, who gurgled happily, and I left my meal to ring for help. Eventually, a charming policewoman arrived, filled in lots of forms, and took the child away. I pondered at the sadness of the situation, but I was even more astonished when the father reappeared at hometime, asking for his daughter back. I pointed him in the direction of the police station and left them to deal with that one.

Mrs Hawthorn was quite the opposite. She couldn't bear to part with her child, and after reluctantly pushing her into the classroom when everybody else had already settled down, she'd stand outside the Reception classroom in tears, waving at Jasmine through the window. Jasmine sat on the carpet sobbing too, until her teacher began to find the sobs tiresome. I cornered mum in the corridor and explained that if she didn't toughen up, Jasmine wouldn't settle at all.

'She just can't get used to Mrs Hills,' she said. 'She spends all her time with me and her nan, you see.' We compromised. She'd bring

Jasmine on time and then stay outside the room for a minute or two. She'd also try to radiate a little happiness and smile at her child.

It didn't work. Worried about getting an inferiority complex, Mrs Hills asked if I'd do the registration and call her when things were quiet. I agreed, only to find that Jasmine howled twice as loud. In a panic, I put the register down and hurried out into the corridor to catch mum. 'What on earth is the matter with her?' I asked. 'Why is she so upset now?'

'It's obvious, isn't it?' said Mrs Hawthorn. 'She's crying because she's missing Mrs Hills'.

6

I am constantly awed by the intricacies of young minds

It's SATs week and, as usual at this time of year, I'm invigilating with my two Year 6 teachers. We've worked hard all this year, putting aside the construction of technological miracles from cornflakes boxes so that we can concentrate on the all important core subjects. I'm anxious to see how the children do, and I realise I'm almost as nervous as they are. I get to school even earlier than usual.

But at 9am the sun is shining, and so are all the faces of Year 6. A beautiful May Monday, and not a single absence. Every one of them is here: the able, the less able, the unable, the unstable. Spurred on by the powers that be, parents have been persuaded that SATs are *very important*, like Ofsted inspections and league tables.

Year 6 troop excitedly into the hall and sit at the individual foldaway tables we've bought. Expensive, these tables, but replacing the worn out library books isn't that important, is it? The children examine their new pencils and unchewed rubbers with relish, we explain the mechanics of SATs week, and the tests begin. The silence is wonderful, and the day passes quietly.

They're all here on Tuesday, too. Even the unable. Especially the unable. Damn it, this could muck up our league table position. Gary's hair has been cut for the occasion, and Jade has a box of perfumed tissues to mop her troubled brow. It's mental maths today, and as I listen to the careful articulation of the voice on the CD I wonder why, just a few years ago, the powers that be were telling us that doing whole-class mental tests wasn't 'good practice'. The voice asks the children to circle the approximate weight of an apple. What apple are we talking about, I wonder? A cooking apple? A crab apple? The children hurriedly scribble answers into the boxes. Just as Haji's facial contortions suggest he's moving towards an answer, the voice moves on, throwing him completely.

We grind through Wednesday, and on Thursday it's maths test B. My wife and I eat the usual quick breakfast before dashing off to our respective schools. 'How much does an apple weigh,' I ask her? 'Haven't a clue,' she replies. I hurry to school to help find the implements needed for the maths test: new pencils, calculators, rulers, protractors. Year 6 are astonished at the daily production of new accessories and study their immaculately sharpened pencil points with interest.

In question two, the children are shown six shapes, all differing slightly, and they're asked to find which one is identical to a seventh shape. The examiners have assumed tracing paper would be helpful and said they can use it. Silly examiners. Nine of the children, who manage to turn their tracing paper upside down and inside out during the process, become totally confused and get it all wrong. Gary wraps his comb in his tracing paper and looks as though he might play it.

But children are adaptable and by Friday they are almost blasé about the tests. I know when they've finished now, because they turn to their neighbours to see how things are going and accidentally knock their pencils off the desks. As they bend to retrieve them, they knock their rulers, rubbers and protractors off as well. I tell them to try very hard not to drop pencils, and immediately three more clatter to the floor. The science test begins, and Mark buries himself in the food chain question. What will happen to the otters if an item earlier in the food chain disappears? Mark thinks carefully. 'Otters might go dark,' he writes with supreme confidence. I am constantly awed by the intricacies of young minds.

At 4pm on Friday I join my Year 6 teachers to pack the SATs into huge bags and post them off for marking. I read aloud the incredibly detailed packing instructions. They involve appendices, manifests, bar codes, and a bag of sticky bits and pieces. I look despondent, remembering this confusion from last year. One of the teachers puts a SATs sack on his head and hums softly in despair. Clare, newly qualified and efficient, finally sorts it all out and our premises officer struggles towards the staircase with the packages. 'These weigh a ton!' he gasps. 'They do indeed,' I reply. 'But I bet you don't know how much an apple weighs'.

7

Carla won't be in – her mum's waters have broken

Another Thursday – for some reason usually the most difficult day of the week – is over, and what's it been like? Some target-setting, perhaps? Browsing the school improvement plan with interested governors? Finishing a new policy document? Chatting to parents about the school/home contract? That's how lots of people might see my job. Reality differs...

8.10 It's pouring with rain. A child, whose parent has long since gone to work, sits under the shed playing *The Ode To Joy* on her recorder. I'm struck by how beautiful it sounds. Carla's Nan waits for me by the gate: Carla won't be in, Mr Kent, because her mum's waters have broken.

8.20 Dave, trusty premises officer, says there are problems with the downstairs staff toilet, and we'll have to call the plumber. Again. We'll need to shut the toilet for the day, Dave says.

8.22 Chat to the teaching staff on the ground floor. One has a dreadful cold, but she's in. Hurried discussion about a child whose attendance is very poor.

8.30 Secretary Sandra arrives, breathless. Her car died in the road. Check diary, open yesterday's post. There's a report from an LEA auditor, riddled with spelling mistakes. Can't anybody write decent English these days?

9.00 The whistle blows, and the children come in happily and quietly. Most of them, anyway. Mrs Elsen and her new partner appear. Peter's lip bled at break yesterday, and they want to know what happened. They also want our school behaviour policy, an apology, and a written account of the incident from the playground duty teacher. They'll collect it later, they say.

9.30 Dave says the middle-floor toilet isn't that great either. It's dripping rusty water from the cistern. It's okay as long as you don't sit under it.

9.40 A note from Andrea's mum. What am I doing about headlice? This is the third time she's mentioned it and no one's listening. I glance at the pile of leaflets and nit combs left by the nurse and destined to go home today. I smile. Andrea's mum will think I've ordered them in answer to her letter.

10.00 Choir. A Thursday highlight. Troy auditions again, but he's got a voice like sandpaper. He fails miserably. 'I'll try again next week,' he says cheerfully.

11.00 Playtime's over. Unusually problem-free, apart from Gary and Hassan arguing again. Gary's cussed Hassan's sister, and Hassan's called Gary's mum a prune. Gary's upped the stakes by cussing Hassan's entire generation, so Hassan's hit him. I administer plasters.

11.10 The architect arrives to discuss window refurbishment next term. Can they do three classrooms at a time? I haven't a clue where I'm going to put the children.

11.30 My time with the nursery. I read Mick Inkpen and overact wildly. They laugh hysterically. Mr Kent's so silly. Delightful.

11.50 Holly and Effan appear, both self-assured infants. Someone's been down Holly's lunch box, Effan says, and nicked her 'choclitt'. I give Holly my Braeburn apple and say it tastes even nicer than chocolate. Holly's impressed and they potter off happily. I make a note about the chocolate nicker.

12.30 Lunch with the children. I look forward to my usual crisp salad, followed by an orange and yogurt. Except the lettuce hasn't arrived, or the beetroot. Or the yogurt. I see what else is on offer. I eat my orange slowly.

1.45 The man arrives to collect library book boxes. I'd completely forgotten to tell everyone he was coming.

2.00 Someone arrives to discuss re-cabling the computer room. I check my diary. He's supposed to be here next Thursday. He checks his electronic organiser. The battery's flat again.

2.10 I find Emit from Reception waiting for the secretary. He's wet himself again. He's sitting on the chair that parents use.

2.20 The LEA consultant who's doing my annual headteacher appraisal rings. Can I send her performance data, development plans, action outlines. Should I send her Emit, too, I wonder?

3.00 My assembly with the infants. My theme this term is the body, and I show them experiments demonstrating how wonderful the eye is. They listen attentively, and I remember what the job is really about. The best bits are always with the children.

3.30 The real part of the day is over. Now, and into the evening, it's the meetings, the budgeting, the policy documents, the target setting, the planning. All the things I'm far too busy to do during the day!

8

The whole place became a mass of jumping, writhing children

It's the school disco, and we've sold a staggering number of tickets. It's also the first time we've had a disco, because I go out of my way to avoid the things. I've given up trying to keep pace with the noises youth listens to these days, and when my daughter's boyfriend asks me which clubs I used to rave at when I was young, I explain that skiffle used to get me pretty excited. He gazes at me sympathetically, and I tell him the music he enjoys would put me straight into an asylum.

But, says the newly formed Parents' Fund Raising Group, discos are fun and nice little earners. They promise to run the whole thing, clear up afterwards, and tell me I don't have to attend if I don't want to. I warm to the idea, especially the thought of raising school fund money, but feel a pang of conscience about not attending. I decide to go. So do my trusty deputy head, secretary, and all the younger teachers. The children talk about the event excitedly, and in four days all the tickets have gone.

The big night arrives and the queue forms dead on 7.30. Dave, Premises Officer par excellence, has already prepared the hall and stands in the corridor behind a large table. Nobody enters without a valid ticket, and since all tickets have been numbered and names jotted down, there's little opportunity for gatecrashers. The disco lights are on and the DJ is testing her microphone above the sounds from the huge speakers wheeled in on trolleys.

Children flood along the corridor and into the hall, filling it with colour. They chatter above the noise and admire each other's clothes, the fashion-conscious circling the hall proudly. Danielle and Stephanie have no trouble chatting several decibels above the music, since during school time they can communicate with each other from opposite ends of the playground. The older girls have applied some make-up, not always with consummate skill, and they move to the music in small friendship groups. The older boys hug the radiators, or eye the girls with slight embarrassment but a little admiration, too.

The DJ tells everybody to get on the floor because we're going to have some fun, and the parents wave their children goodbye for the next couple of hours. I smile at the parents as they leave, to show them what fun I'm having. The lights go down, the decibels rise, and the whole place becomes a seething mass of jumping children. The teachers join in, one of them wearing flashing lights on her head. The children love this, and I pray that Miss won't put her back out or sprain anything.

I circulate with my deputy and we watch the wilder dancers with great amusement. Charlie, special needs, is cavorting and gesticulating around the room like a deranged dervish. Tiny George, Year 3, has smothered himself with his dad's aftershave and it looks like he's got his dad's best shirt on, too, because it down goes down to his ankles. His head moves back and forth to the beat like a pigeon chasing biscuit crumbs. Sarah and Shajna dance in perfect sync – real talent here – until Shajna wheels round and accidentally smacks Thomas in the ear. They look daggers at each other and I move in to calm tempers.

I go to help with the refreshments. We're selling crisps and fizzy drinks and making a tidy profit on these, too. Tony comes back repeatedly for more cups of Irn Bru. He's treating his mates, and the girls as well. Majid asks if we've got tomato sauce crisps. I tell him there's salt and vinegar, beef, and cheese and onion. OK then, he says, have we got any prawn cocktail? I explain again and he buys beef, but only gets three yards before dropping them all over the floor.

When I return to the hall, one of the parent group is leading a lively conga. Arms and legs flail everywhere, and those with least stamina fall by the wayside. Or just fall. The DJ announces prizes for the best dancers and everyone goes wild when the latest piece of loudly shouted incoherent rap hits the speakers, their arms punching the air with pleasure.

The two hours pass like lightning, the children have been delightful, and the event has been an enormous success. They go happily into the night with their parents. Despite the headache, I realise I've enjoyed it too... and the profit we've made will buy lots more instruments for making *real* music...

9

For a while, nobody wrote 'bum' on the walls

Many primary schools are housed in elderly Victorian buildings, and for somebody used to a modern, well-equipped office, the conditions we work in must seem surprisingly primitive. The trouble is, schools are filled with little things called children, and updating ancient facilities doesn't always guarantee improvement.

Consider our new toilets, fitted a while ago after repeated pleadings for a small slice of the LEA buildings improvement cake. For a while, the children were in awe of the newly painted walls and nobody wrote 'bum' on them. There were shiny chromium taps that just needed a gentle push before they cleverly turned themselves off, banishing the previous problem of water wastage when children left taps running. There were brand new pans and lovely clean cubicles. Everybody was happy... and the cleaners especially so.

The euphoria didn't last long. The plungers on the taps still went down quite well, but refused to come up, often sticking in the full-flow position. As the new basins were smaller, a child could achieve a spectacular flood very quickly, by thrusting a bit of tissue into the plughole. More fun was to be had with the new toilet door locks, supposedly designed to work simply and easily. It wasn't long before somebody found that a pencil point would jam the locks from the outside, causing considerable anxiety to the poor soul trapped within. Fortunately, the toilets weren't too far away from the office and the howls of anguish quickly brought the nearest adult or child to the rescue, but it struck me that even the lowliest secondary technology lesson could have designed something better.

Once again, our trusty Premises Officer had to think his way around that, as well as gluing the rubber collars to the back of the ceramic pans, because the toilet physicists had discovered that easing the rubber right back caused the next occupant a real surprise, as he flushed and suddenly found himself ankle deep in water.

However new and high-tech an improvement is, children will always find a way to do something they shouldn't with it. Take the simple device known as a switch. When we had our old, unsafe lighting system removed, new switches were put at the top and bottom of the staircases in our three-decker building. Previously, the switches were operated by key, and the lights turned on by the premises officer at the beginning and end of the day. When they were replaced by ordinary two-way switches, the naughtier element amongst our older children realised there was fun to be had at the end of a winter's day by waiting until home-goers were halfway down the staircase and then plunging it into darkness. It wasn't easy to catch the culprits; if I nipped up the other staircase and moved silently and swiftly along the top corridor like the Phantom, the naughties had already shot to the bottom of the staircase and done the same thing with the other switch. The problem was eventually solved by threats in assembly and the distribution of staff near the switches at home time.

Playground 'furniture', such as water fountains, can be a nightmare. Ours are fairly new and don't get heavily used in the winter, but in the summer there's a perpetual queue, and the nozzles often become slack. With deft manipulation, it is possible to spray the entire queue lightly, or virtually drown the person standing directly behind. Some children become so adept at it, they can soak a shirt at fifteen paces and then apologise innocently to a less experienced teacher on duty, swearing blindly they had no idea it was going to do that, Sir.

When we had a mains burst in the playground, a team of plumbers dug more trenches than at Ypres during the First World War, and the opportunities were rife. Health and safety paramount, the workmen surrounded their trenches with netting, but the children devised all sorts of fun-filled activities, such as seeing how many tennis balls could be landed in the trench before the plumber leapt screaming over the netting, or seeing what the plumber said after being asked 20 times if he'd like a thumb to plug the leak until he'd fixed it, because they'd heard a story about that.

Our windows are about to be refurbished and we'll have scaffolding all round the school. Frankly, I shudder to think of the possibilities.

10

Please Sir, what about an 'orror film?

Like most primary schools, we teach English and maths. And geography and history and science. But, to paraphrase the Wizard of Oz, we've got one thing the others haven't got. Friday Film Club.

When I was small, I loved my weekly trip to the Saturday morning pictures. There, surrounded by schoolmates, I could curl up in my seat, laugh at the comic car chases, be thrilled by intrepid adventurers, howl at Tweetie Pie's antics and, best of all, squirm with excitement at the cliffhangers in the Captain Marvel serial. There was something about the big screen that invaded my senses and has drawn me to the cinema ever since.

During a summer holiday some years ago, I even converted the loft of my house into a mini-cinema, and my own children spent hours captivated by Super 8mm extracts from movies such as Star Wars and Superman, splashed across a six foot screen.

Friday Film Club is my way of bringing the pleasure of Saturday morning pictures to a new generation. We have a room in school called the Viewing Room, where classes normally watch TV and DVDs. I've erected a huge hardboard screen on the front wall which opens out to Cinemascope proportions. Secondhand Super 8mm equipment is inexpensive nowadays, so we've installed a couple of projectors – and a good sound system. The only thing we lacked was a set of cinema seats, but since a lot of children were to be packed into a relatively small space, a thick carpet seemed a better idea. We don't have to hire or buy any films; I've been collecting Super 8mm extracts for years, and I have a library of more than 400 films to choose from.

Each Friday lunchtime, infants and juniors pay their 40p, drop their tickets into a box, and pour into the Viewing Room. Such is the popularity of the show we even had a forger, though his ticket wasn't hard to spot: it was handwritten and the wrong shade of blue.

My young audience knows exactly what it's in for each week; cartoons, perhaps a classic Tex Avery, an extract from an adventure movie, a comedy.. often Laurel and Hardy, Buster Keaton, Charlie Chaplin... and always a Tom and Jerry to finish with, raising a huge cheer as the logo hits the screen. Quite often, I'll also include a short film that makes the children think, such as Norman McLaren's *Neighbours*, or perhaps a small piece of *Fantasia* which is a treat for the ears as well as the eyes. And Captain Marvel is in there too. I managed to find the entire serial in mint condition for a knockdown price at a boot sale.

Watching their faces gazing at the screen in rapt attention always reminds me that children haven't changed as much over the years as we think. A good story is still paramount; special effects today may have reached breathtaking complexity, but a chunk from *The Wizard of Oz* can still hold them spellbound, and the appearance of the witch occasionally causes an infant to move a little closer to one of the juniors for comfort. Similarly, some of the early Walt Disney cartoons like *Bambi* have a timeless appeal, especially on a big screen.

Children have a wonderful sense of humour too; show them Laurel and Hardy trying to push a piano up a huge flight of stairs, or attempting to rig an aerial on top of an unfortunate lady's roof and they will howl with laughter as the chimney collapses.

We've been running Friday Film Club for some years and there have been amusing incidents along the way. When I screened a film taken in the front car of the Blackpool big dipper, the screams of terrified laughter brought several teachers running from the staffroom to see if everything was under control! The youngest and smallest infants often demand that I show some "orror films', and since I'm a great fan of the early Universal series I obliged by running an extract from The Invisible Man. My teachers appreciate the club as it gives them an extra 10 minutes at lunchtime on Fridays, though when I ran an extract from *The Young Ones*, an older teacher, a huge Cliff Richard fan, came dashing in to watch.

I can't, of course, justify Friday Film Club in terms of targets, achievement tracking, or performance management. It's fun, pure and simple, but fun seems to be an increasingly rare commodity in schools these days

11

Cheryl is a coat loser of Olympian quality

As the last week of the summer holiday fades away, I mentally travel the ups and downs of the past year, just as I do every September.

Still, only two years to retirement. Not long at all. I remember the horrors of the window refurbishment, the way we ploughed on through dust, dirt, constant hammering and sawing, workmen delighting the children by swearing loudly when they hit a problem, the annoyance of moving classes out of their rooms every five minutes, and having the building shrouded in plastic during temperatures that shot off the thermometer. But not only did my wonderful teachers plough on with grim determination, we achieved our best SATs results ever. Perhaps we ought to have the windows refurbished every year.

I remember the aggressive parents. You always remember the aggressive parents. Only three this year, but aggressive encounters stay with you for days. I remember Anthony's dad in particular, a fearsome gent with eyes pointing in opposite directions and a permanent sneer. He charged in on a wet Monday morning, demanding to know why Anthony's teacher had made fun of him and kicked him off his chair. It took half an hour to calm him down, and another two meetings before he realised his son had made up the story, probably because he liked winding his dad up and pointing him in the direction of the school.

I remember the piles of lost clothing. Expensive coats, jumpers, jackets that children leave everywhere apart from the peg with their name on. Cheryl in particular. Cheryl is a coat loser of Olympian quality. Give her a new coat and she'll lose it by playtime. Along with her lunchbox. And her earrings. Even if she gives her earrings to the teacher while she's doing PE, she loses them as soon as the teacher gives them back. It runs in the family, because her mum often loses Cheryl. She'll wander all over the school at hometime calling her name, and Cheryl will be wherever her mum isn't.

I remember the horrifying water bill. How had it shot up by three thousand pounds compared with the last one? A quick look at the water meter in the road revealed an arrow spinning round like a yo-yo on a string. Urgent calls to a plumber... and the unwelcome news that we seemed to have a major leak under the playground. Might mean having the entire playground dug up, but the water company does refund most of your money if you report the leak. Usually. Still, if my budget goes haywire, I'm retiring soon.

I remember the expense of repainting the toilets, hoping that the children would take more care of them. They did, for two months, until somebody scrawled 'sex me up Charlie' into the paintwork with a pair of scissors. And the toilets reminded me of the day I was visited by the leader of the religious group using my school on Sundays. He came to thank me, and he came bearing some very odd gifts: a cellophane wrapped face flannel, some religious colouring books, and three plastic bags full of toilet rolls.

And that, in turn, reminded me of the summer play, and the poor infant who was caught short while jammed into our small hall with the rest of his class. He didn't have time to rush outside. God knows what he'd eaten, but his bowels had given up the struggle. Fortunately, it was only the dress rehearsal.

But I remember, too, delightful and deeply fascinating moments. Georgia singing solo in the school play, her voice captivating us all; Siva placing a large packet of chocolate digestive biscuits on the dinner table, saying his mum had given him packed lunch money so this is what he'd bought; the delights of Poetry Week, our best ever, and the pleasure of the staff at seeing our children so enthusiastic about something that might last into their adult lives; Tashi writing her own 'Greek myth' which was as good as anything a fifth-former could produce; Andy inventing a guitar run in the middle of my guitar lesson and the others applauding, open-mouthed in admiration. And tiny Emefa from Reception, slipping her hand in mine as I walked down the corridor and telling me how much she loved school and chatting to me. Not for much longer though, because I'll be retiring soon.

Maybe.

12

Rain seeped through the usual seven places

Although it isn't a major part of the primary curriculum, I've always felt that drama has enormous value for children. For ten years, my music co-ordinator and I have written musicals, and drama activities have formed an important ending to each term. It is something the children work hard at and look forward to. At Christmas, every child is involved in the concert, and at the end of July there is the summer musical. Each teacher and class contributes in some way; there are songs to be choreographed, pieces of scenery to paint and props, programmes and advertising posters to be made.

The show has become a tradition, and more ambitious as the years have passed. The children show such interest and enthusiasm that even the auditions last for days. When we wrote a new version of Hansel and Gretel, the finalists for the part of the witch were so good I chickened out and asked a group of children to choose for me. A large cast is assembled, and the atmosphere builds as rehearsals go on throughout the summer term. The final performance, held in the evening, is a gala occasion, and no child has ever missed the show.

We've had our moments, though. Producing the show is a doddle compared with handling the parents on the big night. Our hall is relatively small, it's often hot in July, and we pack them in. The first problem arises with getting the parents, some of whom are rather large, to the top of our building. They battle the staircase, groan when they reach the top, and ask me weakly when I'm getting a lift installed. Then a parent governor, always chosen for her ability to give parents a withering look if they don't sit exactly where they're told, jams everybody into rows of upper junior chairs, which aren't really suited to the size of the bottoms they're asked to support.

Once everybody's seated, the audience is shown how to fashion fans from the programme sheets. It's an amusing moment, but my young cast suffers more; they're stuffed into costumes and work under stage lights as well, always without complaint. And despite the newsletter saying parents mustn't bring babies to the show, a handful always appear and I wait, tentatively, for them to start crying. You just know it'll be during a quiet scene, and the mother will be squashed in a row at the back, causing the child to howl loudly for the two or three minutes it takes for the mother to extricate herself from the hall. But there's a huge pride about the event too; when one of the younger children was chosen as the show's star, her mother brought both her current boyfriends to watch the performance.

Just occasionally there have been moments when I wonder if I can stand the tension, such as the evening a mother turned up smelling of alcohol and sat down heavily behind a younger woman. The show had barely started when the inebriated woman began accusing the younger woman of sleeping with her husband. A fight started, and although I wasn't able to reach them, a young male teacher manoeuvred them to the exit and was kneed in the groin for his efforts. Despite the shouting that continued all down the stairs, the cast only hesitated momentarily and then flung themselves back into the performance.

On another occasion, we'd been delighted that the night was so cool... until torrents of rain hit the roof and began seeping through the usual seven places – and on to the audience. Teachers hunted for bins to pass among the crowd, and for fifteen minutes the show was accompanied by the loud clonking of rain against metal. The coin collection afterwards was our best ever, one parent stating that her fiver might not buy a new roof but at least it would pay for a couple of slates.

A few infants have fallen off the stage when they've become immersed in their acting, but we've only ever had one real accident. Tony played the evil magician, and was doing wonderfully until, in the darkness between scenes, he decided to give the scene shifters a hand. There was a cry of 'Mind me foot!', a loud thump, and for the rest of the performance the magician had a pronounced limp, which got steadily worse. After the show, I suggested his mum might pop him down to casualty, just in case. The next day, she told me that Tony wouldn't be back for a while because he'd broken his foot and it was in plaster. 'I could hardly get him home,' she said. 'Mind you,' she added proudly, 'he was bloody good in his part, wasn't he?'

The show must always go on.

13

Will the prisoners kindly
leave the dock

I'm not going to school today. In fact, I won't be going into school for the next two weeks.

I'm on jury duty and, since I've been called to the Old Bailey, I'm bound to be watching skilful barristers summoning vital pieces of evidence at the eleventh hour, freeing the defendant to the sound of gasps from the public gallery. You know, *Twelve Angry Men*, Charles Laughton in *Witness For The Prosecution*. That sort of stuff.

I reach the station with time to spare, pleased to be out of the usual traffic jam. The platform fills so rapidly that I'm in danger of being edged on to the track, so I move backwards discreetly. The train arrives and every inch of every carriage is stuffed with bodies. I nudge sideways and commandeer two square inches by the door. Good thing I started that diet last week.

A strident female voice demands that the man in grey moves down the car, because we've all got to get to work, haven't we, and would he kindly use the two empty cubic centimetres to his left. The man shuffles with embarrassment and three more people pile in. The doors close and I can't move at all, so I study the ear of the sardine next to me until we reach London Bridge. By the time I've fought my way to the Old Bailey on the underground, I feel better disposed to traffic jams.

More queues at the Bailey. We must remove metal objects from our pockets and squeeze through a scanner. I'm called back and I search for anything remotely resembling metal. I can't find a thing, so the attendant helps. The culprit is the metal foil on my pre-diet Rolos. We're handed subsistence claim forms and a swipe card to pay for lunch. Then we're divided into groups, ushered into various court rooms, and told by a clerk to sit towards the back.

When everybody is seated, the clerk asks if the prisoners will kindly leave the dock. It's a little joke, but a hostile, middle-aged female voice informs him she has arthritis, and if she wasn't to sit in the dock she can't think why he didn't tell her which bit was the dock before she sat down. I wonder if she's the sister of the lady on the train. The clerk, thrown by this from his usual patter, makes one more attempt at joviality. 'Don't leave your belongings lying around,' he says. 'There might be some thieves in the building.' There's little response to that either, so, glumly, he switches on the training video.

We're moved to the waiting area. It's hot and congested because two big cases are starting. Another clerk edges to the microphone and tells us the law is a funny thing and we'll probably spend a lot of time sitting around. Then he calls out our names from the register, and I instantly remember all the things I forgot to remind my deputy about. The clerk stumbles over a very long Indian surname, and there's a burst of laughter when a cockney voice shouts, 'Yep, I'm 'ere, mate!' I join another long queue, buy a plastic cup filled with plastic tea, and take paper and pen from my pocket. I might as well sketch out the first scene for the summer play.

Soon, I realise that all the people round my table are teachers. The table becomes a staffroom, and everybody says how useless their headteachers are and wouldn't it be wonderful if heads got to know some children instead of producing daft bits of paperwork. There are vigorous nods of agreement and I slink further into my coat, trying desperately to look like a chartered accountant.

The microphone crackles and my name is called. A crisis at school? No, my name is the first to be called for a group of jurors and I join the other names outside. My Henry Fonda role is within reach at last. We're asked if any of us has connections with the police, and I say my nephew is a policeman. I'm told I won't be able to go on this case, and return to the waiting area, carefully avoiding the staffroom table. I scribble hard on my pad and at 2.30 I'm dismissed for the day.

I'm dismissed at 2.30 on all the other days as well. I don't get on a case, I don't see Charles Laughton trounce the opposition, and the diet's a bit dodgy because a cream bun or three has brightened up the tedium. Still, at the end of it all, I can claim £23 subsistence. And I've written three scenes of the summer play.

14

Watch out, here's Threshold Man

I was clearing my filing cabinet the other day, and I came across last year's Threshold Assessment folder. My mind drifted back to how angry I felt when the idea was first introduced into schools.

After six years, a teacher reaches the top of a pretty unexciting salary scale, but to earn any more, he or she must move on to an 'upper' pay scale which members of other professions would find mean. To have a hope of crossing this 'threshold', hoops must be jumped through and evidence collected. Headteachers, never trusted by the powers that be, weren't allowed to assess this evidence, even though they knew their teachers better than anyone else. An army of consultant assessors was recruited to march into schools to pass, or fail, the poor souls whose knees trembled with worry over whether their forms would pass muster with a stranger.

Expensive to set up? Well, the video had to be prepared, of course, and tons and tons of paperwork, and a website created and set up, and all the special forms for the local education authorities all over the country. And then there was the recruiting and training of the assessors. It wasn't actually too taxing to become one. So long as you had a couple of GCEs and a certificate saying you were in the scouts and could tie a reef knot, you were on. A few hours training made you fully competent in deciding whether a qualified teacher, who had trained for years and then spent at least six more in a classroom perfecting her skills, could do her job properly. And you wouldn't have to use your own initiative; the DfES had put questions on tick sheets and even helped you with what you were supposed to say. The cost of setting this up? Well, what's £25 million among friends? Your average consultancy could easily spend half of that preparing a paper on why chalk isn't the best medium for writing on a white board.

I remembered the half-term week my wife spent with a group of colleagues, sitting in our lounge frantically justifying themselves for Threshold Man on bits of paper. I ministered coffee and sandwiches to keep them buoyant, and listened to the earnest and worried conversations as they questioned each other and wondered if what they'd written would get them through. And I remember thinking how utterly demeaning it all was – any competent inspector need only spend two minutes in their classrooms to appreciate their commitment and ability.

Before long, it became harder to recruit Ofsted inspectors than threshold assessors. I've often wondered what makes anybody want to be an Ofsted inspector anyway, but it seems shorter hours, an easier workload and good pay caused the inspection army to shift camps. One consultant admitted to me that threshold assessment was 'a bit of a gravy train'. I lived in hope that one day a maverick attendant would shift the points and cause the train to carry the gravy into schools instead. Even the guide for headteachers was patronising. 'Promptly notify all teachers of the outcome of their application' it said. Well fancy! I hadn't thought of that!

During its first year, seven of my staff were eligible for the threshold. Two found the forms so patronising they threw them in the bin. One found the whole idea objectionable and said sod the salary increase. Another two waited to see what would happen as this new system got under way. The remaining two found it objectionable as well, but both were single with high mortgages, and teaching salaries don't lie easily with London property prices. They were two of the finest teachers I've worked with, and great friends with each other, but at one point the threshold process came close to damaging the relationship.

In typical fashion both teachers had prepared boxes piled high with work examples, statistics and topic folders. The problem came when one saw that the other not only had one more box than her, but had also labelled her items in a particular way. Her face clouded over. 'I thought we'd agreed not to do that,' she said testily. 'Now I'll have to change mine as well.' I knew it was momentary tension, but I was angered at the ridiculous process causing it.

And what's happened now? Well, the army of consultants has moved elsewhere. The schools and the government couldn't afford it, and headteachers now do the appraising. Shame they weren't allowed to do it before the 25 million was wasted...

15

I won't have people wagging fingers at him

Consider these scenarios.

One: a teacher of 30 years who believes children thrive in a structured environment with clear discipline guidelines takes detention on Tuesdays. One Tuesday, a child disrupts others by talking constantly. He is asked not to – several times. The teacher steps outside to break up a corridor fight. When he returns, he finds the talker dribbling into his coffee mug. He grabs the child's arm and calls him a dirty little boy. The parents complain about the 'manhandling' of their son, and the teacher's inappropriate speech. The teacher is suspended for a short period because it's the second time he's touched a child; two weeks earlier, he'd stood at the top of a busy and dangerous staircase keeping the children moving. A child had deliberately walked in front of him and the teacher 'steered' him in the correct direction.

Two: At playtime, a teacher realises she has not locked her classroom and on her return she catches a child taking money from the class savings tin in her desk. She tells the head, who calls the parent to school. The parent tells the teacher her son is not a thief. He told her that he was looking for a rubber, and she believed her son, so why didn't the teacher believe him?

Three: the whistle blows at the start of school. Children are lining up to go into class. A top infant is fooling about, making faces and refusing to take his place. He is showing off in front of his mother. The class teacher wags her finger, telling him not to be silly and to get into line. The mother hurries over and says her son is not silly. Moreover, she won't have people wagging their fingers at him and she will report it to the headteacher.

The three incidents all happened recently, the first to a departmental head at a secondary school, and the others in my own school. I'm sure many teachers will sigh and say incidents such as the last two happen every day, and incidents like the first one are becoming increasingly common. But that doesn't mean we should accept them.

We live in an age when authority is challenged and teachers no longer have the respect from parents that I enjoyed in my classroom career. This is why we have to toughen up to it, and why heads and senior managers, while being fair, must go out of their way to support their colleagues. In the first scenario, why was the teacher not supported? The child was in the wrong and it should have been made plain to the parents that if they didn't support the school they could take him elsewhere. My school is in a difficult area, but we won't accept bad behaviour. Everyone has to have the same standards and every teacher needs to believe there will be adequate back-up if there is an incident.

Some schools have Parent/Teacher contracts. Personally, I don't think they're much use, because parents who bother to fill them in will be supportive anyway. I think it is essential that people who are senior managers in schools set up a relationship with the parents of unruly children early on, establishing mutual trust. If a child is disruptive in class, it is unfair to the ones who want to work, and *their* parents have every right to complain, too.

It's a sad sign of the times that I have to explain to my newly qualified teachers that their classes are likely to give them grief simply *because* they're new. And, unfortunately, so will some of the parents – for the same reason. I explain how important it is to create a disciplined working environment from the first day. You can always pull back later. Then I watch them make the same mistakes we all made.

One young teacher, creative and inspiring, started her career with a difficult Year 6 group. She listened to my warnings, but she wanted to be a friend to the children. She chatted with the naughtiest ones at playtime, thought she had 'won them over' and then couldn't understand why they behaved badly when they were back with their mates. She tried advice given by her college tutors, many of whom hadn't taught for centuries. I supported her as much as I could but she had to grind her way through the rest of the year.

By her second year, however, she knew what she wanted and her class wasn't given a moment to waste. Gradually, she cultivated a class of lively, responsible young people. They knew and understood the boundaries – which all children need and want – and had total respect for her. By year three she was stunning.

Ultimately, it pays to say 'Don't do that!' and really mean it.

16

Unfortunately, £7.32 seems to be unaccounted for

Well, the auditor's gone. It's daft really, but I view the auditor's visit like a trip to the dentist. You try to keep your teeth in good condition, but there's always something wrong.

I really don't think auditors understand how many jobs a headteacher has to finish in his average day, or how many talents he's supposed to have at his fingertips. After all, an auditor just audits. He knows the shape of his day and what is likely to happen. It doesn't include Charlie throwing up on his carpet after falling off the playground bench, or the tea urn breaking down again, or Mrs Smith hollering because a playground supervisor dared to wag a cautionary finger at her naughty little boy.

I'm not cut out to be an accountant, but in our brave new educational world, these skills are expected of me in abundance. When I became a head, my time was spent doing the things I considered important: shaping the curriculum, teaching drama and music, helping teachers develop their skills, mounting work displays and exhibitions, spending time with children and their parents, and ensuring children had access to a variety of exciting activities. Wondering whether the school could afford a few extra pencils was the local education authority's concern, not mine.

Nevertheless, because managing the money is mandatory nowadays, I've found there are aspects I enjoy. Setting out the budget, for example, and deciding how we'll organise it, or discovering there's enough money to develop an initiative we've toyed with. I like making sure the money is well managed throughout the year, and there's a certain satisfaction from emerging in the black by a few pounds. I enjoy watching my bursar account for every penny on his monthly visit, because I couldn't do it, even if I spent a year with the books on a desert island.

Computers make things simpler of course, but technology can be a hindrance, too. Years ago, when heads were told they would be managing their own budgets in future, we were given a computer, an exceptionally unfriendly accounting package, and two day's training. Almost immediately, there were disagreements between various departments of the local authority because the reports produced by the package were fine for the finance department, but not for the auditors. A second package was bought in from elsewhere and linked into the first one. Problems mounted when the bits of software refused to co-operate with each other.

In desperation, at the end of the second month I took the paperwork to the 'experts' at the LEA, and I got in the queue with the other heads and administrators who were trying this last resort before shooting themselves. The experts couldn't work it out either, and in the end I decided to stop worrying about it. Soon the existing package was junked (at what cost, I wonder) and something more sensible bought in.

Nowadays, things run pretty smoothly, but I'm still wary of the auditor. I prepare for his annual visit like my teachers prepare for an Ofsted. I put out all the books, files, reports and expenditure details with care and precision. I label and list everything. I give him a room and a chair and two chocolate biscuits with his tea.

Nevertheless, I know exactly what is going to happen. 'I've selected a few things at random from your stock book of audio visual items,' he'll say, 'but the 19-digit serial number on the black and white portable television doesn't match the number in the book. The Casio keyboard bought in 1972 doesn't seem to be where you say it is, there are only 19 headphone sets, not 20, there isn't a receipt for the £3.50 Miss Thompson spent on postcards when she took her class to the

Tate, you've used your Barclaycard to buy a computer, and out of the £1,200,000 the school spent last year, £7.32p seems to be un-accounted for.'

I offer explanations. The telly doesn't work, the missing headphone set was taken to bits by a child, Miss Thompson was an NQT and forgot a receipt, the computer was a bargain and wouldn't have been available the next day, the Casio moved classrooms, and does seven quid really matter? The auditor smiles and says he understands the pressures, but he has to go by the Ofsted recommendations.

Ofsted recommendations? Well, that explains it.

17

A barrage of sludge shot into the corridor

We've had our school windows replaced. Well, refurbished actually, apart from those so weather-beaten they were nailed shut in case they fell out of their frames. We'd sweated pounds during previous summers without fresh air, and rejoiced when we heard the LEA was coming along to sort us out.

Naively, I'd assumed the LEA would arrange for a firm to do what I'd done to my house: remove all the old windows and replace them with tough white plastic ones closely modelled on the originals. Then, unlike the wooden variety, they'd probably last until the building fell down.

But it wasn't as simple as that. The responsibility for decorating the inside of the building (including the window interiors) lies with the school, while the LEA looks after anything to do with the outside. And since some of the windows in the more sheltered sections of the building weren't disintegrating, only the worst ones would be replaced. By the time the contract was signed, the outsides were to be refurbished and the insides untouched, unless the insides were damaged while they were refurbishing the outsides, in which case they'd touch up the insides. With me so far?

After an extended half-term holiday while the school was covered in scaffolding, the work began. The LEA had decided that the brickwork should be steam-cleaned while the scaffolding was up and, to stop muck flying everywhere, the building was shrouded in polythene. And thus our troubles began. The building became like the Palm House in Kew Gardens, but you couldn't see out of any window to know whether the sun was shining or the rain pelting down. Since we'd had more rain last year than Noah, runners had to be organised every few minutes before playtime to check if the children could go out. When the wind blew, the polythene flapped like the wings of the mythical Roc, making it difficult to be heard in the classrooms.

But worse than this was the brick cleaning machine, which made a fizzing, high-pitched scream. If it was outside your room, teaching became impossible. You could guarantee that if you moved out of your class for the morning, the next bit of wall to be done would be outside the room you'd just escaped to. Several times I'd just started assembly when the machine fired up, drowning out my voice. It amused the children; they began to think the workmen were doing it deliberately. After a while, so did I.

Nothing seemed to have been co-ordinated. When we stopped for playtime, the workmen stopped, too. When a class moved to a different venue while the scraping and painting was done, it always seemed to be half-finished when it was time for the class to return. You could be in the middle of discussing the parts of a plant because SATS were approaching, and two workmen would wander along the planks outside your window, discussing in colourful language how many pints they'd downed last night. Another workman removed the nursery door in the morning, offering an escape route for 25 small children. He left his Black and Decker plugged in on the bench by the door. It only takes one inquisitive little finger.

My premises officer, determined that the work wouldn't go on a moment longer than necessary, watched the proceedings like a hawk. He's so good-natured it's hard to get him upset, but he refused to budge when a workman drove up with a bald tyre and no tax disc. And I did feel sorry for the painter who accidentally knocked a guitar off its hook in the music room and damaged the tuning pegs; Dave pursed his lips, shook his head, and told him it was the headteacher's own instrument and cost £600.

Don't the worst things always happen on Friday afternoons, though? The muck from brick washing clogged a drain in the playground, and one of the workmen had a bright idea. Since they had a high pressure hose with them, it would only take a moment to shift the blockage. Unfortunately, the playground drain was linked to the one in the infant toilet, and a barrage of filthy sludge suddenly shot around the toilet walls and into the corridor. Dave nearly had a heart attack, and had to hire outside help to make the place habitable again. Thank God there were no children in the toilet at the time. What on earth would I have told the parents?

18

An earthworm would be OK.
Or a crane fly

I have a soft spot for guinea pigs. But I hadn't had much contact with them until my youngest daughter asked if she could have a pet for her birthday.

Life in our household is exceptionally busy, so I wasn't keen on a dog or a cat; you need to walk the former and be home in time to feed the latter, so I suggested alternatives. An earthworm would be OK. Or a crane fly. Or a couple of goldfish. Undaunted, she insisted we visit the pet shop and there, bright-eyed in a cage with two rabbits, sat a baby black guinea pig. It was just old enough to leave its mother, but young enough to fit into your palm.

My daughter was delighted, and we drove home with the animal, a large cage, water bottles, hay and a guinea pig service manual. He was dubbed Sam, handled every day, and soon lost the nervousness that is characteristic of these lovely little creatures.

It's often thought that guineas don't do much, but Sam quickly proved the exception. We were decorating at the time, so he was given a free run of downstairs. For warmth, my daughter laid a blanket made from pink and blue patchwork squares beneath the radiator in the hall. To our surprise, he spent the next few days chewing out all the pink squares and leaving the blue ones intact.

Sam liked entertaining us; he'd follow my wife round the room, and stop when she did. We'd put him on the floor, and he'd bolt round the skirting boards until, worn out after three frantic circuits, he'd sit behind the curtain peeping out in case we put him back in his box.

Guinea pigs need to keep their teeth short, and they'll have a crack at chewing most things. Sam viewed the house plant we'd been growing for years as a rare delicacy, though he knew from the tone of my wife's voice it was strictly out of bounds. It didn't stop him, though; once, after a cautious glance at her, he stood on his back legs to reach the lowest leaf, reached too far, and performed an ungainly somersault that surprised him so much he spent an hour beneath the radiator, staring out moodily. We only got cross with him once, when his chewing wrecked the phone line, internet and TV aerial in one evening. It was remarkable that he hadn't had a shot at the mains.

He was rarely ill, though he did catch mites, which began destroying his fur and made him itch. He looked very sorry for himself as we covered him with lotion and dunked him in a bowl of warm water, but he was a hardy little soul and he survived four more years, keeping the grass under control and chatting to squirrels, cats and the occasional fox cubs that came and sat on his run. We buried him, aged six, under our lilac tree, the blossoms tinged with my daughter's tears.

Soon, we had two more. Identical twins this time, and we named them Tony and Simon. It was a cold winter and we brought them in at night, popping them into straw-lined washing baskets. When one tried to sleep, the other whistled loudly, until Simon discovered he could leap out of his basket and land in Tony's. When we separated the baskets, Simon leapt out and hid behind the settee, daring us to chase him. Tony was more of a Colditz pig, not realising he could simply climb out of his basket if he wanted to, and spending his evenings trying to burrow out instead. I assumed he was a special needs pig.

I showed them to the children in assembly. They were fascinated, particularly when I sat them on separate PE stools and they whooped at each other across the hall. The children must have gone home and talked about this, because the same week we were offered two females by a parent who was unable to keep them. We were delighted, and we put them in the Nursery class.

One morning, premises officer Dave stopped me as I came into school. 'I'm a bit worried about those pigs,' he said. 'One of 'em's really heavy. I don't think they're both females.' Shortly afterwards, a large litter was born, and Dave set up home in his garage for the constant stream of children and teachers itching to admire the babies. Finding homes for them wasn't difficult, especially as Dave and his wife decided to keep two. I watched with pleasure as a non-speaking nursery child became attracted to the pair, increasing his vocabulary daily as he tended them and found words to describe them.

Oh, I forgot to mention that our Sam turned out to be a Samantha. That must be why she preferred the pink squares to the blue ones.

19

There'll be a new initiative in the next five minutes

How's performance management this year then? Shaping up? Lots of meetings with willing teachers as they reflect on their achievements and tease out fresh targets? Finding it blindingly exciting and a sure-fire method for moving your school onwards and upwards? No? I thought not.

But help is at hand with *Mike's Bluffers' Guide to Performance Management*. If you're an overworked head, this is for you. If you're not, photocopy it and slip it on to your head's desk. It's designed to allow teachers to do what they're employed to do. Teach. Here we go...

Impressing the Inspectors: Ofsted teams and local inspectors (or School Improvement Advisers, as they're currently known) often forget what children are, so you'll need the numbers and percentages routine to impress them. Gather some well chosen phrases and learn them by heart. Try: 'Yep, PM has certainly shifted our percentiles. Did you know that the mean averages of our upper quadrant have shot up by 0.2 of 3 per cent in attainment target 3 for children with ADS? Shows what selective targeting can do, eh Brian? Got a few hours to study the graphs?' Brian will nod wisely, thank you for tea, and tell you he's late for his next appointment. He won't visit for at least six months.

Impressing the School Governors: Most governors are public-spirited folk with a desire to help. They also appreciate how Canute felt, as they try to stem a flood (paperwork, these days) that they don't understand and can't control. And when they do spend a late night wading through an initiative, another one arrives in the post the next day. They decide the best thing is to leave it to the head (since he's sorting out this stuff every waking hour) and nod knowledgeably at the next meeting.

The tactic, therefore, is to show the governors the huge model performance management document devised by the DfES, watch their faces as they realise they might have to read it, and then show them the new, improved version you devised with your deputy last night. It'll only be four pages long, but it'll contain all the legally required stuff. The governors will congratulate you and go home relieved and happy.

Impressing the Parents: Parents' requirements are simple; they want their offspring to develop a love of learning in a friendly, safe environment with teachers they trust and respect. If they can contribute to their children's success, they see that as a bonus. The Government, of course, takes every opportunity to broadcast the wealth of initiatives being put in place to get teachers off their bottoms and shake up the schools, performance management being one of them.

Therefore, as you smile at Cynthia bouncing out of the Reception class at hometime, her mother just might ask you what this performance management thing is all about. Bring out the huge DfES document, show her how complex it is, and complain that Cynthia's teacher could spend more time hearing her read if she wasn't spending hours grappling with this garbage. Cynthia's mother will agree, and tell you she wouldn't have your job for all the tea in China.

Impressing the Teachers: This is important. Your teachers are a dedicated, hardworking team, right? Ask them to write down three personal objectives for the year on the last page of your revised document. Collect them, photocopy them three times to make a huge wad of paper, put it in a prettily labelled binder, and file it with the others. Then let your staff get back to what makes teaching the most fascinating job in the world... creating an exciting, stimulating classroom that children love being part of.

Then, during the course of the year, visit them a lot. Talk to them about their careers, their interests, their futures. Make sure your door is always open. Let them choose courses to go on, but never push them unnecessarily. Give them your time, and encourage them constantly. Develop their enthusiasm and don't worry about their faults; you've got faults, too. Teachers are your most treasured resource, and if they love working in your school, the children will love it too.

What they instil in the children will last a long time. Performance management won't. It's just an initiative. There'll be another one along in five minutes.

20

There's a lot to learn, apparently, about managing

I've just had one of those days that make you glad to be a head-teacher.

I spent a delightful afternoon working with children on the school play, Danielle from the Reception class has become a reader, and read twice to me, and we had a productive staff meeting with every-one relaxed and happy. Yet I know that if I were applying for a head-ship today, I'd never make it.

It was easier 20 years ago. Yes, I'd been a successful deputy, and was known to the local authority, but headship applications in London consisted of two short interviews – one with school governors and another at County Hall. All I can remember is being asked about discipline. I said then what I think now: get it right in the infants, employ good teachers who value continuity of behaviour as well as curriculum, and 'discipline' won't be an issue. These days, I suppose I'd have to waffle on about the virtues of circle time.

That's assuming I got an interview. Two of my teachers have become deputy heads recently, and I'm amazed at what they've been through, though it's helped me to train others taking the promotion route.

First, you get yourself on a variety of management courses. There's a lot to learn, apparently, about managing. Then you complete a lengthy school application, posting it off with your computer-designed CV. If you're lucky, you'll be shortlisted. Next, you're invited to the school for a senior management briefing. Wow! You'll hear where the school is at and where it's going. You adopt a look of studied concentration, laugh when a joke is made, and trust your body language says you're the only one worth considering.

Then there's the tour of the school. This is essential, because it gives you a chance to run from the building if children are throwing chairs and the teachers are smiling desperately. But no, all seems fine, so it's on to the presentation, a modern feature that even applicants for curriculum posts have to endure. If you're a computer whizz and the school is into ICT, you'll whip out your laptop and plug it into the electronic whiteboard. Away you'll go in PowerPoint, animating bullet-points across the screen and reiterating them verbally for those who can't read.

Now it's on to the buffet lunch with selected staff and governors. Much of your time will be spent balancing vol-au-vents in one hand and warm white wine in the other, while decoding what Mrs Foster-Ladsbury means when she asks how your target-setting informs your planning.

But you're a good mixer and things go well. Now the formal interview, held on another day – which means you have a chance to mug up on that day's DfES initiatives. Here's where the battle is really fought, and you're anxious not to make a slip. You crawl out after the grilling and drive home wondering how you made such a mess of it. Then the clerk phones and, if you're successful, it's a truly wonderful moment. If you're not, you start all over again. I can't imagine how awful that must be.

I'm not certain the current system is that much better than the ancient one that appointed me, and I worry that senior management is too far away from 'the child' these days. I appointed my deputy because she was a delightful person, an efficient organiser, and able to create a stunning classroom environment.

I still think those are the things that matter most.

21

Can't he paint a picture
or something?

The other day, we were bemoaning the amount of time we spend working for the SATS tests.

We want good results, and you have to keep up with the pack. And don't all the other schools cram too? You can't afford to be left behind. When I was a child, in my last year at junior school, the teacher spent most of her time preparing us for the 11-plus. And as a young teacher, I was required to spend hours showing my 11-year-olds how to crack verbal reasoning tests. Yes, there was an interesting lull in the anti-test seventies and eighties, but anything went then, and some children, usually in deprived inner city areas, didn't learn very much at all. Overkill, in the form of a new government, a national curriculum and oodles of expensive testing arrived to sort all that out.

The trouble is, SATS affect other year groups as well. Schools are worried about leaving everything to the final year, so there are now practice tests for Year 5. Even the last two years of primary school might not give enough time to master the art of putting tracing paper over shapes to see which two make a square, so hadn't we better design our own in-school SATs for Years 3 and 4? I sometimes think primary schools are fast becoming factories with the sole aim of getting everybody out of the building with a level 4.

There are knock-on effects, too. Ofsted inspectors seem to use SATS as a litmus test for everything. Before the team arrives, the reporting inspector will have pored over graphs and percentages from all the data you're required to upload to the internet these days, in your detailed Self Evaluation Plan and lots of other time consuming forms designed by government VDPs (very dull people), purporting to give a picture of the school in miniature and not doing anything of the sort.

Then, having found the tiniest weakness in your Year 2 SATS for 1835, where the graph trembled because very able Daphne had moved to another school and your best teacher had annoyingly gone off to have a baby, they'll home in to show that your school is falling apart. Even local school inspectors use these bits of paper religiously. Every year, when the delivery man risks a hernia getting SATS boxes up the stairs, my stomach lurches at what it must all cost. Even the instructions for sending the tests off are unbelievably detailed and must have been written by a huge committee for days on end.

Parents have been persuaded that SATS tests are vital. In my school only two children have ever been absent for them, and one was only away for a day. Once the lift in a local block of flats broke as five of our children were on their way to school for the start of SATS week. Three were terrified. Not because they were stuck, but because they might miss science 'A'.

And yet the SATS results don't matter to the children. They've already got their secondary school places, the schools have been informed about their abilities, and the parents are aware of how their children are progressing because the teachers go out of their way to inform them. They matter to the school though. My God, everybody, we've slipped two places down the league tables. We're coasting. Or failing. Next stop, special measures, and then they'll close us down.

But I had to smile when a mother approached a friend of mine, and asked if she could give her 11-year-old some extra lessons a couple of times a week. 'SATS practice?' inquired my friend. 'No bleedin' fear,' she said. 'He gets that all day long. Can't he paint a picture or something?'

22

Clare's experience haunted her for weeks

Please draw your chairs closer to the fire; I'm going to tell you a horror story.

When I employed Clare, not so long ago, she proved herself a talented, dedicated teacher. After three years she wanted to travel, but she was a teacher through and through, and I guessed it wouldn't be long before she was back in a classroom again. When she returned, she enlisted with a supply agency and her first assignment was a day with a Year 5 class in a leafy suburb.

She was directed to a hut, cut off from the main school. Surprised to find she had to shout to be heard, she was told by the 'behaviour monitor' that misbehaving children had to write their names in a box on the board. The child then had ten minutes to improve, whereupon the name would be removed. Unfortunately, she wasn't told what happened if the behaviour didn't improve.

Warren, a large boy, began to fool about. Clare asked him to put his name in the box, and he refused. She asked again. He stood up, kicked his chair, and swaggered to the front, deliberately knocking books off a display. He stared at Clare, wandered into the cloakroom area, banged the door, and then made faces through the window.

Other children now began to show off, too. Clare scribbled a note to the head, asking Andrea to take it quickly. She didn't even reach the door. Warren leapt in front of her and shoved her back. Unnerved, Clare ordered him to sit down. Still punching Andrea, Warren walked up to Clare and screamed 'No!' in her face. Then he turned and started fighting two other children, saying he would only sit down if Clare didn't send messages. She told him she did not bargain, and was here to teach, not referee.

Warren knew that Clare had no way of getting help. Again she tried. Immediately, Warren jumped on the child she tried to send. During the commotion, the classroom assistant was able to run to the office, but there was nobody of any seniority available.

Eventually, the regular class teacher arrived back for lunch from the course she was attending, and reluctantly told Clare she'd sort out the problem using circle time. She managed to lower the noise level, and asked the children to explore their anger and examine their feelings. Warren remained defiant, and the headteacher was summoned again. She was irritated to be called, and warned the children she 'might have to talk to their parents'. Warren raised his hand and asked her if he could have a bag of pins, explaining that he 'wanted to stick 'em in the other kids'. The class teacher urged Clare to stay, so that she could return to her course, and, after eight children had been removed, Clare staggered through the day. The experience haunted her for weeks.

Some teachers now experience this daily. It is no longer extraordinary. But these children were 10-year-olds, and reaching the end of what should be an enjoyable chunk of their education. What have we come to, that children can be so uncontrollable at such a tender age? What chance has the secondary school receiving these children got? Precious little, I suppose, except to expel them.

Yet I remain cautiously optimistic, because it doesn't have to be like that. Perhaps the first step is to train senior management to be hands-on leaders, not people who hide in barricaded rooms under piles of paperwork.

23

On Tuesday, the alarm suddenly goes off...

We have a shiny new fire alarm.

I listen in awe as the electrician proudly explains the high-tech console that controls the red glass-panelled boxes screwed to the wall. It's a shame that so much of the children's work has had to be ripped off the walls to fit these boxes, but that's high-tech for you. It worries me that the boxes are within the children's reach, and one is perilously close to the juniors' playground exit.

On Tuesday, the alarm suddenly goes off. It's an incredibly piercing sound – worse than Year 3's first descant recorder lesson. I come out of my room to find teachers in the corridor, their bodies vibrating. Then the noise stops as suddenly as it started. I hurry to the control console, where premises officer Dave has switched it off. Meanwhile, two teachers have discovered Mary (Year 4, special needs) standing sheepishly near a little red box with its glass broken. Her brother George is beside her. George is into high-tech. He looks at me carefully. 'Me sister dunnit,' he says.

Next day, I'm running the lunchtime film club in a room full of infants. The fire alarm goes off. Teachers emerge from the staffroom, puzzled. A fire drill? Should they go outside? Should they fetch their registers? Aaron is discovered – his mates having grassed him up. Aaron didn't mean to do it; he just happened to be waving his arms around when he hit the funny little box. At the following day's assembly I explain the importance of treating the new alarm with respect. I read The Boy Who Cried Wolf, and the children listen intently; the message seems to have struck home. At 3.30pm, it goes off again. By now, the staff have almost come to expect it, and I have a sinking feeling in the pit of my stomach.

The bell rings interminably. Dammit, Dave is at a premises officers' meeting, so I open the control box myself. I stare at the flashing console, but it might just as well be the flight deck of the Starship Enterprise. What did Dave say? Turn the key twice, pull the lever across, push a button. After five permutations, the noise stops. Meanwhile, a parent governor has cornered Andrew by the playground gate. Andrew left us last year. He swears he leant against the button by accident, with the innocent expression he'll no doubt use to tell the judge he was only borrowing the motor to do some shopping for his gran.

The following week, I call the electrician. Could he remove this particular box? There is a sharp intake of breath. Difficult, with this new high-tech system. It would mean some wiring adjustments and he'd need permission for that. And there's the expense. Could it, then, just be put out of the children's reach? Another intake of breath. It *could*, but you've got the same wiring problem, and what if a child discovered a fire?

The alarm goes off again at 2.30pm the next day. I rush downstairs to find a quivering delivery man in the corridor. He tells me he was just unloading netball equipment and he smashed the glass accidentally and Jesus doesn't it make a racket.

Later that day, when I eventually get home, my wife tells me that a neighbour a few houses away has been burgled again, and we really should think about getting an alarm. The nearest DIY superstore has one on special offer, and it's late-night opening tonight if I fancy popping up there....

24

Millions are wasted on flawed initiatives

For more than 20 years now I haven't been a class teacher, and, although I love my job, I miss the pleasures of daily contact with a class. And if I were in a classroom today, I wouldn't run it too differently from the way I ran it all those years ago. I'd want it to be a stimulating place, filled with colour and interest. I'd want my pupils to enjoy coming to school. I'd want them to interact positively and sensitively, and to feel what they were doing was worthwhile. And I'd want every child to feel the excitement of acquiring knowledge and fulfilling whatever potential they have.

I've met hundreds of teachers during my career. Virtually all share those aims. Like me, they get up early, get to school early and work hard all day – and often during evenings and weekends. But then, teachers always have. Which is why I was irritated by a statement from a government minister earlier this year stating that the government's focus on forcing up standards is changing education year on year, with the 'dedication and commitment of our teachers now delivering real improvement'.

Have teachers been twiddling their thumbs for years without getting anywhere, and have they suddenly seen the light under the current administration? I don't think so. Leaving aside the less than helpful funding, the constant blaming for society's ills on schools, the wasting of millions on flawed initiatives, the ever-changing curriculum and the constant demands that we appraise or performance-manage ourselves to destruction, just consider any aspect of the primary school curriculum and look at how it trundles around in expensive circles.

Take literacy. When I first became a headteacher in the eighties, misinterpreted Plowden techniques were in full flow and every mark a child made on paper was celebrated with whoops of joy. Reading schemes were out, as was structured learning. Children were supposed to choose books themselves and learn to read by osmosis. Grammar or phonics teaching meant you kissed promotion goodbye. Funny how those who bulldozed these methods into schools were careful where they sent their own children to be educated.

Secondary schools received children who could barely write their names. In private, primary teachers admitted unhappiness with the methods forced on them. Many, worried about children's achievement, used reading schemes and hid them when the inspectors descended on their schools.

Then the national curriculum appeared... but teachers, bruised and battered by the insistence on 'child-centred' learning, were wary of suddenly lurching in another new direction. The Government picked up its sledgehammer, and a 'literacy hour' was expensively born, insisting on grammar, phonics and teacher-led sessions.

Battalions of inspectors and advisers ran around checking that things were done in the way the DfES video told you to. (Funny how they always showed tiny classes of immaculately behaved children.) But we've lost something vital. I became a writer because I was inspired by teachers whose enthusiasm and excitement about literature made me want to try it. And looking through the mountains of achingly dull 'literacy' crammers in W. H. Smith's last week made me wonder if primary schools will ever be allowed to travel a sensible, middle road.

25

We'd completely wasted one of the busiest days of the year

I remember my first September as a headteacher.

I went into school frequently that first summer holiday, nervous but excited by the prospect of shaping my own school. I just hoped this headship thing was going to keep me busy. Looking back on 25 years of the job, how naive I was. There was no headship college in those days, and little advice of any note, but nobody could have prepared me for the intensity of the job and those moments of insanity that occur regularly throughout the year.

Take the last Thursday of this summer term, for example. We have a security storeroom containing the safe where secretary Sandra keeps the various monies that flow in and out. The safe has two enormous padlocks. She has keys to them, and so do I, but there are no others. Just before assembly, Sandra was in her room looking worried. 'I've lost my keys,' she said. 'It's annoying because I need to get the end-of-term accounting finished.' By the end of assembly, she was even more worried. 'I've checked everywhere,' she said. They've vanished.' Since three classes had gone on school outings, I wondered if one of the teachers might have picked them up by mistake. We found their mobile numbers, but none had seen the keys.

Sandra thought for a moment. 'Perhaps I've locked them in the safe. Can I borrow yours?' Sod's law was fully operational that morning. The safe keys were on my Mini key ring, but the Mini was on my drive waiting for me to give it a new clutch, and I'd brought the Clio to school. Nevertheless, I didn't live very far away and I could nip home and fetch the keys... until I remembered that Andrew's dad, who gives my Clio a professional valet every six months, had taken the car.

Never mind, Sandra could run me home. But her car keys were on her key ring with the safe keys. And the teachers who had cars were all in their classrooms, teaching. Enter premises officer. 'I'll nip round the DIY and get a hacksaw,' he said. 'We'll have to cut the locks off.' After twenty minutes of energetic sawing on the huge padlocks, Dave estimated getting through both of them would take just under a week. 'There's a quicker way,' he said. 'I'll fetch my angle grinder.' He returned looking annoyed. 'I can't find the cutting discs. I put them somewhere safe. I just need to remember where.'

Enter Donna, a teaching assistant whose husband also owned an angle grinder. 'He's at home today,' she said. 'I'll pop over and get it.' When she returned, I held the first padlock in a large pair of grips, and Dave attacked it with the grinder. Sparks flew. 'Let's hope we don't set anything alight,' Dave grinned. 'If anyone sees us, they'll ring the fire bell.'

Three minutes later, the fire bell rang. Children, teachers, helpers, kitchen staff poured along the corridors, wondering why we were having a drill right at the end of term. Dave hurried to the alarm control box, and I sent everyone back to their classrooms. Darren owned up to setting the alarm off. He'd always wanted to break the glass in the little red box, and this seemed a legitimate opportunity.

By the time we'd cracked the safe, we'd wasted one of the busiest days of the year. There was a time when I'd have panicked at the amount of work left to do, but not any more. I'm an older and infinitely wiser head. Oh, and Sandra's keys were in the safe, after all. But she made lots of money on our last raffle, so we're OK for another couple of padlocks.

26

The ultra-reliable failsafe immobiliser had failed

Energetic members of my staff cycle to school but, like many teachers, I rely totally on the car because it carries much more than a pile of exercise books: the cage for the guinea pigs, props for the play, equipment catalogues and so on. I have a mint condition, classic 1987 Mini Mayfair, and it runs like a sewing machine because I service it myself. When I lift the bonnet, I can find the spark plugs, the oil filter and the distributor. I can put a dab of white paint on the crankcase timing marks, attach a strobe. Engine tuning's a doddle. It's what Sunday mornings used to be about.

But modern cars are different. Servicing? Pop into your dealer every million miles, sir. Apart from that, just fill it with petrol and drive.

Recently, we needed a bigger car – partly because the weekly shop is tricky in the Mini, and partly to cart my daughter's baggage to and from university. Lifting the bonnet on our new Ford reminded me how much cars have changed. I recognised where the engine was, but the rest had me mystified. 'Don't worry,' said the salesman. 'They're very reliable these days. And this one has a really sophisticated immobiliser. This tiny key handles eight engine functions.'

And it did, for two years – until the time we went to a wedding. I pushed the tiny key into the dash. Everything bleeped and flashed like the Starship Enterprise, but the car wouldn't start. I opened the bonnet, hoping for divine intervention, and then in desperation suggested we pile into the Mini, which got us there crumpled but punctual. The next morning, I climbed into the Ford, rolled it back in gear, and it started. 'Aha!' I thought, 'The starter motor's jamming.'

But reaching the starter motor was impossible, so I popped the car into my friendly local mechanic. He rang me later to say that the starter motor was perfect, and the engine started every time. I fetched the car, and put it on the drive.

The next day, it wouldn't start – so back to the Mini, which would. After school, I rocked the car in gear again, and it fired straight away. Mystified, my mechanic checked again. 'I've had the starter motor out and greased it,' he said. 'I've checked the electrics and I still can't find anything. It seems fine.'

And it was. Until the day we went to the seaside and it conked out in the pouring rain. This time, no amount of rocking would start it, so my wife went off to find a phone and get help. It occurred to me that we might have to catch a thing called a train. I wasn't sure I'd recognise one – and dammit, the inspector was visiting tomorrow, and I had that special needs meeting at 10am. I turned the key almost absent-mindedly, and the car started.

Nothing for it. It had to go to a Ford dealer, and I took an hour off school (unheard of, for me) the next day. That evening, the mechanic said he'd tested everything. It started every time, he said. No problems at all. He turned the key to prove it. The car wouldn't start. Astonished, he phoned a top Ford electrician, who promised to visit the next day.

And then, success at last. It seemed the reliable, failsafe immobiliser was failing – when it felt like it, when it rained at the seaside or when we had to get to a wedding on time. Like a surgeon, the electrician removed the immobiliser and its intricate wiring, and since then it's started like a dream. Modern technology is great when it works. But you know which car I drive to school?

The 1987 Mini Mayfair.

27

Sorry, but Steven doesn't know which way up a book goes

I'm glad I'm not a special needs teacher. And especially glad I'm not a special needs co-ordinator.

When I became a head in the dinosaur era, special needs teachers were, well, exactly that. They helped children who needed it most, working in small groups away from the classroom. The idea was to hone children's basic skills, give them a sense of pride and achievement, and then get them back, full-time, amongst their classmates as quickly as possible.

The teachers who do special needs work haven't changed much, but their role certainly has. These days, the children come a poor second to the paperwork, but it has to be done, immaculately, if the school is to receive additional money for pupils with the greatest need. Indeed, some special needs co-ordinators spend all their time form-filling, or nagging overworked teachers about handing in termly special needs reviews and 'individual education' plans.

Parents are becoming ever more demanding. I never cease to be amazed by the number who never chat to their children, read to them, or listen to what they have to say – and then insist their children are dyslexic and in need of extra help. The poor special needs co-ordinator is hurled from pillar to post coping with the bureaucracy – and that's when the parents are being co-operative.

It's a nightmare when they're not. My special needs co-ordinator works part-time, but teaches most of the hours she's in school, preferring to do her paperwork at home. The children adore her, the special needs workroom is colourful and exciting, and her under-achieving children make very quick progress. Perhaps that's what keeps her going, because her trials and tribulations with adults and the local authority have to be witnessed to be believed, and her patience on the telephone in my office often causes me to stop working and listen in rapt admiration.

'Hello, is that Mr Ahmed? Oh hello. It's Ms Doyle here.' Pause. 'Ms Doyle. You know, Amid's special needs teacher.' Pause. 'Yes, Amid's teacher is Miss Jones. But that's his class teacher. I'm the special needs teacher and I give him a little extra help. You were supposed to come to a meeting this morning.' Pause. 'Well, it was a meeting with the educational psychologist. And you. And me.' Pause.

'No, Amid isn't sick. The educational psychologist can help us to get some extra support for Amid. You promised you'd come. Psychologists are very busy but I've managed to get one for half an hour...' Pause. 'We can't get support for Amid unless you discuss it with us.' Pause. 'I think you did know about the meeting. I've written three times and spoken to you twice on the telephone. Aren't you worried about Amid?' Pause.

'Yes, I'm sure he is very helpful in the shop. But he can't do lots of things that an eight-year-old should be able to do.' Pause. 'No, I don't think hitting him with a big stick would help. Could you pop round for 10 minutes, then? ' She sighs deeply and puts the phone down.

I'd have given up months ago, but Kathy won't. The child, not the parent, is always in her sights, and I admire her for that. Only one parent has ever defeated her, and I sat in the meeting while she outlined, in detail, her concerns about Steven to his adoring father. 'You do realise,' she cautioned, 'that Steven doesn't even know which way up a book goes?"

His father smiled serenely. 'Well,' he said, 'show me a five-year-old who does...'

28

You're the headmaster? So why you drive this little Mini?

Primary school life is full of little rituals. Each day I perform several. Come rain or shine, I wander into the playground for the last 15 minutes of the lunch hour. I can help calm any troubled waters, but there's constant pleasure and amusement to be had from watching and talking with children. Take yesterday, for instance.

Katie runs up. 'You know that music you played in assembly? My dad likes John Williams too. I've got some CDs upstairs he said you could borrow. And there's another one he said you might like. It's by – she thinks for a moment – 'Vague Williams'. I explain that I love Vaughan Williams and I'll be playing some of his music in assembly too.

Vladislav, recently from the Ukraine, is looking thoughtfully at my car through the gate into the car park. 'You are the headmaster of this school?' he asks. I agree that I am. 'Then why you drive this little Mini?' he asks. 'You should drive a big car, and the other teachers a small car.' I promise to sort out the travelling hierarchy of my staff and he looks at me quizzically before wandering off to philosophise with other Year 6 children. They back off as he approaches.

Jamin tells me there's 'rude writin'' in the toilet. I call Cedric and Tunji over. They're my toilet wall troubleshooters. They shoot off for the damp cloth and Cif bottle, knowing there's a free film club ticket if they can remove it before the whistle.

Kieran spots me and hurries over. Kieran is adopted. He was assaulted by his natural parent, and school hasn't been easy. He takes out the two conkers his adoptive dad has strung on shoelaces and gives me one. A small crowd gathers. They cheer when I bash Kieran's conker.

Gladys asks if I'll watch her friends perform. They line up, adopting poses of the latest pop group to savage the charts. The girls sing of unrequited 'lurve' and their bodies gyrate with the pain of it all. They get a round of applause and ask if I want to listen again. Diplomatically, I explain that I'd better check the other bits of the playground. A football bashes into my leg and Luke apologises profusely, which is rare. Had I been a child, there would have been a shot of vitriolic abuse and I would have been harangued for being in his way.

Selim is in the park area, studying nature. He has a microscope at home and he often stands for inordinately long periods staring at leaves and things. In class, where there isn't an abundance of leaves and things, he stares at the ceiling instead. He's found a black and white ladybird on a bush. This is unusual and interesting. He carefully puts a leaf in an empty crisp packet, and pops the ladybird inside. I don't fancy the ladybird's chances, but I could have a budding biologist here.

I ask Molly if she's taking her violin home for the weekend, but she says her mum wants a break. Her mum says even the budgie's bought ear plugs. Three girls run past, shouting at me to stop Alan chasing them, but obviously loving every minute. Chasing girls is Alan's current pastime, but he's overweight and the exercise won't do him much harm.

The whistle blows, the footballers chant 'We won!' and the children line up. No fights today, not even an argument. Probably because it's sunny and there isn't any wind.

But just wait till the weather changes...

29

Washing your cup is a smart and achievable target

There's a problem I can't solve, one of those burning issues that teams from the Department for Education are sent abroad to study.

Let me say at the outset that my teachers are marvellous. They're hard-working, humorous, never off sick, and totally committed to their job: a real pleasure to work with.

But they don't wash up their cups.

The staffroom has a huge Butler sink, there's no shortage of water, and years ago the cups would be washed and lined up neatly on the table beside the sink. But in those days, washing the cups was a 'primary helper' job, and helpers have now become classroom assistants. They no longer have to wash cups, so the cups sit in the sink.

When the problem first appeared, my deputy wrote a notice saying 'Please Wash Your Cup' and stood it at the back of the Butler, but the only thing that got wet was the notice. In no time at all, you couldn't read it. So she made another and tacky-backed it. The hot water curled it up.

I put a polite note in the staff notice book asking if people would be kind enough to wash their own cups. Nobody else's. Just their own. Just the one. But still the Butler bulged.

And then the problem suddenly broadened. A teacher who was leaving bought a set of cutlery for the staffroom. It didn't stay there long; teachers would hurry in at lunchtime, fetch what they intended to eat, and wander off to mark books with one hand and eat with the other, taking the plate and utensils with them. Most plates were usually retrieved, some from the oddest places. I found one on the window ledge in the toilet, which, if nothing else, goes to show what busy people teachers are. But where do I find the remaining plates? With the knives and forks in the Butler.

Then one morning I found the sink bleached and the crockery stacked and sparkling beside it. I thought new leaves had been well and truly turned. But no, the cleaner had looked at the state of the Butler every evening, couldn't stand the pile of unwashed crockery, and worked her way through the lot. Undoubtedly, I thought, the staff will be impressed and feel guilty. Two days later, I realised my optimism knew no bounds.

Once again I put hints in the notice book. Eventually I ran out of subtle quips; and the Butler ran out of space. My deputy sighed despairingly, rolled her sleeves up, and set to work after school. I suggested we buy 25 white mugs and write people's names on them. Then we'd catch the culprits. She pointed out, gently, that people would just use somebody else's.

We agreed it should become a major agenda item at the next staff meeting. Performance management and target setting would have to stand aside while we debated this burning issue. Nobody, of course, owned up to not washing their cups, but there was a wide variety of alternative ideas. A dishwasher, someone suggested. Good idea, I said. The only problem is that somebody needs to stack it. And unstack it. And add rinsing fluid, and salt. Washing your cup isn't a gargantuan task, I said, just a target. Smart, and achievable. Could we try once again? We agreed we could.

I'm writing this a few weeks into the new term. And I'm just off to empty the Butler...

30

Good guitarists never hold their dinner money while they're playing

Today I started another beginners' guitar group.

We have 48 guitars, and most children who want to try can, but the first lesson is always a nightmare. I put guitars beside each chair and the children come in excitedly. They choose a chair, pick up the guitar, and hammer away at the strings, mentally becoming fabulously wealthy pop idols.

A guitar at the back seems to be playing itself, until I realise it conceals George, the tiniest lad in the juniors. I suggest a smaller instrument. Tunji and Cedric, inseparable, sit next to each other. Cedric tells Tunji how his uncle plays an electric guitar. Tunji's impressed, until Cedric says that a string snapped and broke his thumb. Tunji's face drops, and he wonders whether he should join the gardening club instead. Busola, a boisterous girl with a deep voice, has started to sing as she strums. The child in the next seat grimaces and I call for silence. Everybody except Busola and her partner stop. Eventually, she catches my eye, and tells her partner to shut up because Sir is trying to talk.

The first trick is to get the group to point their guitars in the same direction. This entails knowing left from right, which catches a few children on the hop. It's why I put out the chairs for the first lesson myself, keeping several metres between them. When children manoeuvre guitars, tuning pegs can easily end up in somebody's nostril if it isn't done carefully.

At last, we're all playing on the same wicket and I introduce the parts of the guitar. 'These are the strings,' I say. 'Don't play them for the moment.' Immediately, somebody does. 'Sorry, Sir,' Spencer apologises. I forgive him and then I tell the children I'm going to say a very rude word to describe a part of the guitar. They look up eagerly. 'This,' I say, 'is the belly.' They giggle and repeat the word softly.

I introduce some science to the lesson, explaining why the sound hole is important. There is a clattering noise; Faye has dropped the change from her dinner money inside her guitar. The other children are fascinated and wonder how I'm going to get it out. I explain that good guitarists never carry dinner money while they're playing.

The sunlight is strong, and George discovers he can bounce light off his instrument into Georgia's eyes. Science again. Other children try, until I explain that we're here to become Segovias, not Newtons. I explain how a note is produced and I say we're going to learn 'E', because it's easy to play. I demonstrate, and the children have a go. It's easy to spot the children who are going to be successful; the less able are having difficulty finding the right string, and a thumb to play it with. George gives up and bounces light again.

I ask them to play eight 'E's in a row, to my hand claps. I count them in, but several play before I stop counting. I try again. And again. I wonder how we're going to progress to the next stage, where they have to use a left hand finger to hold a string against a fret. Then, the lesson is over. They hang their guitars on the hooks and file out, pleased to be heading for stardom. I wonder why I do this every year.

The next group comes in. They've been learning for a year. They pick up their instruments and we break into a lively rendition of 'Blue Moon'. It's great, and I remember that this group, just a year ago, were identical to the group that's just filed out.

31

I bet you don't know my Nan's name

I've given up making new year resolutions. After all, I stopped smoking 28 years ago and I eat sensibly, so what's left? Though perhaps I could persuade the parents who don't collect their children on time after school to make a resolution instead.

Take Clyde and Raine's parents, for example. Clyde and Raine come bounding into the office. Clyde is Year 1, Raine is in the Reception class. Clyde clutches a crumpled animal mask he's made that day. His sister holds a painting. Secretary Sandra rolls her eyes and mutters, 'Not again...'

You can't help liking Clyde and Raine, but an hour of their company can be pretty wearing. We wonder if that's the reason their parents don't collect them. They run to Sandra's desk, as usual, Clyde holds up an animal mask he's made, and the Pinteresque dialogue begins.

Clyde: I made this tiger mask in class today.

Me: Wow, that's a good mask. I bet I can guess what it is.

Clyde: Go on then.

Me: I bet it's a tiger.

Clyde stares at me, astonished: Yeah! Ow did you know that?

Me: Because headteachers know everything.

Raine: I bet you don't know my Nan's name.

Me: Yes, I do. It's Ermintrude Codsbottom.

Raine giggles uncontrollably: No, course it ain't.

Me: Go on then, what is it?

Raine: Dunno.

Me: What's your Nan's name, Clyde?

Clyde: Dunno.

Raine: E don't know much. My Nan says 'e's as thick as two short planks. Can I go toilet?

Sandra: Hurry up then.

Raine runs along the corridor. When she returns Clyde looks at her quizzically.

Clyde: Where did you went?

Raine: Toilet.

Clyde: Can I go toilet?

Sandra: In a minute. So why isn't Nan coming to meet you? Or Mum. Or Dad? Where's Mum today?

Clyde: In my house.

Me: Where's that?

Clyde: Dunno. Can I do some colourin'?

Sandra: Where do you think Mum might be?'

Raine: She might 'ave gone to me Nan's.

Sandra: I'll try ringing your Nan.

Raine: She got cut off. Can I have a biscuit? I'm starvin'.

And on it goes, until, at 5.20pm, I've had enough and attempt to phone social services. I get the engaged tone. I try again five minutes later. And ten minutes after that. How did I guess it would still be engaged?

Suddenly, there's a commotion outside. Mum has arrived, sheepishly beckoning to her children from the corridor, hoping she can get away with it one more time. I hear her apologising to Sandra.

'Sorry,' she says, 'me and their dad was asleep. We just woke up.'

Sandra, very cross indeed, demands that she waits and sees Mr Kent. I draw myself up to full, tired, smouldering height. It's been a long day.

'Do you realise, madam, that it's half past five, my wife is waiting for me to visit her in hospital, my daughter's car has broken down on the M1, and I'm supposed to be taking the cat to be neutered? Once more, just once more, and I won't let your children inside this building.'

It's all bluff, of course. But she hasn't been late since.

32

A profanity too far

I saw a film last night. It was fucking awful.

Are you shocked? No, not that the film was awful. Shocked that I said it was fucking awful?

That's the reason I walked out of it, you see. I'm a movie buff, and the film had been reasonably well reviewed, but it seems you can't watch an adult film these days without everybody saying fuck every ten seconds.

I remember the first time I heard it in a film and, yes, it was '18'-rated ('X' in those days). It was used only once, which is why it had particular force, but the audience sat up in astonishment, and then laughed nervously because we all realised another boundary had just been crossed.

Nowadays, an '18' film isn't a proper 18 unless it's peppered with fucks, and I pine for the days when you could watch a strong adult drama without half the dialogue being given over to one word. Was the strength of the dialogue years ago diminished because nobody said fuck? Of course it wasn't.

Nevertheless, I suppose it's a gift for the screenwriter. After all, you only have to write half as much dialogue. The rest can be filled in with fucks. 'Where did I put my car keys?' simply becomes 'Where the fuck did I put my fucking car keys?' Taken to its logical conclusion, in another ten years Daddy Bear may well be asking who the fuck has been eating his fucking porridge.

When my eldest daughter was studying drama in the sixth form, I remember going to an evening show put on by the students. They'd taken a current news theme, and split into groups to dramatise situations around it. Part of it was scripted, the rest improvised. The fresh-faced youngster introducing the event said: 'I'm afraid we're likely to be using the f-word tonight.' There was a whisper of inevitable acceptance from the audience of parents. I wanted to shout out 'Why?' And I still wanted to shout it out after the performance.

Fortunately, my school playground isn't yet a hotbed of profanity because the children know how strongly we feel about it. But things are changing.

The early morning playground suffers from it, possibly because the children don't think I'm in yet, or that sound doesn't travel up to my window. The playground supervisors at lunchtime are subjected to most of it, particularly during a heated game of football, whereas the children do at least hesitate at morning playtime if a teacher is within earshot.

But then, can you blame them? Many of their parents swear a lot, often at them. Just as they watch their football idols gob on the grass, so they gob on the playground floor in emulation. Switch on the telly after 9pm and the language in most dramas is likely to have a fuck or two somewhere along the line. It is accepted as part and parcel of being 'adult drama'.

There may be a 9pm watershed, but how many of our children are actually in bed by then? And most of them have TVs and videos in their rooms anyway. Even if they don't watch adult drama, I'm amazed at the videos they get hold of, or the number of parents who couldn't care less what their children watch.

I'm certainly not advocating our children exist on a diet of Sunnyside Farm – heaven forbid – and Pete and Dud's Derek and Clive albums always amused me greatly.

But sometimes when I settle into my cinema seat and a stream of invective hits the screen in the first two minutes, even one fuck seems a fuck too many.

33

Sorry, I'm snowed under with paperwork

I might not know the names of every infant in my school, but I certainly know all the juniors, and parents are often surprised by this.

The reason is simple. I spend an awful lot of time with the children. I visit their classrooms, I talk to them, and I teach them. But I'm constantly amazed by the number of primary headteachers who never teach any more. After all, they must have started in the classroom, and if they hated the job, presumably they'd have left to become chartered accountants or something.

It's as if, having reached the elevated position of headship, they never feel the urge to teach again. The less they teach, the less they want to, until the point is reached where any old excuse is trotted out to avoid contact with children. Here are the common ones.

1. Sorry, I'm snowed under with paperwork
Of course, the pile of mail each morning can be large, but much of it can go straight into that finest filing cabinet of all, the waste bin. Especially the stuff addressed to 'the managing director' or 'the chief buyer', from firms who presumably haven't a clue what a school actually is.

Other mail will be from the DfES, or the local education authority, often a questionnaire thought up by some bright spark with two hours to kill before lunch, or the latest ethnic codes for the computerised pupil returns, now running to a total of 8,243 and could you input the whole lot by Friday please.

A shrewd head can whizz through the post in minutes. Or explain the workings of the waste bin to his secretary, so that she can whizz through it instead.

2. Sorry, I've got to rush off to a meeting

A classic and much used excuse. These heads are never in their schools. In fact, their schools are usually falling apart while they're attending meetings about driving up standards. They attend every possible cluster meeting, working party or steering committee, and have lots to say because they are practised at Parkinson's Law tactics... making sure nothing is resolved because then the meeting can spawn lots of other meetings to rush off to.

Courses and conventions are even better, particularly if it's a three-day jaunt at a seaside hotel, paid for out of the school budget, to listen to an obscure expert expounding on balancing perspectives in the divergent curriculum. When they return to school, any chaos can be blamed on the deputy and other senior managers. After all, those people should relish a bit of practice for headship...

3. Sorry, I have to finish the behaviour policy

This is the typist headteacher. The one who sits at his or her computer all day producing endless documentation for staff to read. It's all written at great length and, yes, I'd love to see a child but I simply don't have time, and you just don't understand the pressures I'm under. You can't get in to see this head. Parents have to book appointments weeks ahead. I've even known a typist head who had a light outside her room which would change from green to red. If you knocked when it was red, you'd had it as far as promotion was concerned, and it only went green at 10.45am, when it was time for a helper to wheel in some tea and a cream bun.

4. Sorry, I've got some very important visitors

Useful excuse. Schools often have visitors, ranging from the attendance officer or prospective parent, to a school governor or an inspector. The inspector is a particularly useful visitor, because you can keep him chatting for ages and no one will come anywhere near you. I remember a visit from an immaculately suited, pompous inspector soon after I'd got my headship. There wasn't a great deal of money in the school budget, so I was at the top of a ladder painting the hall walls and I suggested he might like to roll his sleeves up, grab a paintbrush, and give me a hand. He only stayed twenty minutes.

Heads who retreat from the chalkface are missing out on the real pleasure of the job. Even after 25 years, I consider my daily contact with children essential, and I teach the equivalent of a day and a half every week.

I wouldn't change it for the world.

34

Targets – that's the word these days

Call me cynical, but you can't help wondering what the next buzz word will be. We've worked through a few in the past decade or so. It wasn't so long ago that every teacher's lesson, every school governor's agenda item, or every group discussion had to have a 'focus'. If you were a student teacher in school on your teaching practice and you missed the word focus out of your lesson plans, you were in very deep water when your tutor visited.

And then 'share' became the fashionable word. If the inspector called to look round your school (in the days before they came in bundles and were labelled Ofsted), he offered to 'share' some thoughts with you. He meant that he intended to run through your school's good bits and bad bits, just like he'd always done.

And what about 'mission statement'? A truly stupid phrase that caused me great amusement. I associate the word 'mission' with the armed forces, NASA, and Tom Cruise's impossible one, but not with education.

Once, presumably at the whim of a government suit, every school in the land was required to write a 'mission statement'. No longer could your prospectus tell parents about the exciting things going on, nor could you make the assumption that a parent with even half a brain could work out from reading it what your aims were. No, you had to start with a mission statement, and you invariably opened with: 'We aim to develop every child's ability to the full.'

Throughout the UK, every school mission statement was virtually identical. After all, you'd hardly say you that *weren't* trying to develop each child's ability to the full, would you? I remember visiting a school which had it's lengthy mission statement blazoned in huge letters along the entrance walls. Further along the corridor, I could see four older boys beating up a first year...

But targets, well, they're something else. For starters, governors in primary schools are required to predict what the children will achieve by the time they are eleven. Masses of computerised school data will have been collected to help them, but governors are voluntary workers and it's down to the headteacher to do the real spadework, (taking his valuable time away from doing something useful, like widening the school's musical curriculum).

As we're dealing with children, and not sales graphs of potatoes, results are often difficult to predict, especially for the required two or three years hence. In my neck of the woods, families tend to move in and out of the area constantly, and once, when I sent our targets to the education authority, they said I'd set them too low. I pointed out that I was actually making an accurate prediction because the cohort wasn't especially able, and was quite likely to change during the year anyway. Immaterial, I was told; the government had demanded a minimum level from the local authority. I couldn't help wondering if a looming election had something to do with that.

Even so, some of the advice emanating from government circles these days convinces me the writers haven't been near a classroom since their own childhood, if they actually had one.

Silliness has become high art. We're advised, for example, to set different kinds of 'target *zone*': historic, challenge, unlikely or comfort. We're told we should have appropriate data in different years for 'evaluating unexpected variations'. We're told our targets should be SMART: specific, measurable, achievable, realistic and time-related. In some schools, teachers are even asked to set individual targets for every pupil. One assumes they're not expected to teach as well.

When I sigh and show my deputy the latest piece of claptrap for schools, she smiles and tells me not to worry because the latest wheeze will soon be forgotten and things will change in a few months.

And, reassured, I put it in my folder marked 'Documents Assembled For Teachers'. Or DAFT for short.

35

A continually changing agenda is a real turn-off

A friend of mine teaches in a primary school which seems the essence of everything approved of by officialdom. It has top management, senior management and middle management. There are mission statements, planning meetings, appraisal sessions, lesson evaluations and lots of documents, and everything is monitored in detail. Plus, it's in a pleasant, leafy catchment area. The LEA loves it, but the people at the coalface – the teachers – constantly drift away. Sixteen have left in the past three years.

My school is identical in size, but in a very deprived inner city area. It is popular, and heavily oversubscribed. I have a small core of teachers who've been with me a long time and know the school and its environment intimately. We talk about ways to keep moving forward, issues affecting the school, problems we're encountering. Often, we just talk about education.

We don't meet regularly; we're too busy with the job. Middle management? No fear. Why do we need that? Top management? Sort of. If I'm worried about something I'll chat to my deputy in her classroom after school, because problems need to be resolved quickly and fairly. We've never had difficulty recruiting staff, and the only teachers I've lost are those who have moved home or gone on to deputy headships. The atmosphere is exceptionally pleasant, the children and teachers work happily, and our SATS results are far higher than the ones achieved by the leafy school.

My entire career has been spent in primary education, and I've loved it. But when I look back, and think about the constantly changing fashions supposedly improving the way we educate small children, a tinge of cynicism creeps in.

I'm all for things that make a difference, but changing fashions are a constant turn-off for would-be teachers. Schools are almost encouraged to be businesses, obsessed by data, charts, targets, value-added percentages, league tables. We must plan lessons down to the tiniest detail, and never deviate from our plans. All this is frequently forced on us by people who've never taught, or who've escaped from the classroom because they couldn't do it anyway.

Three times a year, I'm visited by my LEA inspector, known these days as a link adviser. He's a pleasant man, but apart from checking up on my school occasionally to make sure I haven't gone berserk and eaten the contents of the sand tray, he is also required to peddle some of the dafter documents produced by the local authority and central government.

Before his last visit, he sent me a document, now used by many LEAs, designed to help us evaluate how good our school is by using 'self-evaluation performance indicators'. The document has 90 pages and, as I thumbed through it, I wondered why it's deemed so necessary to patronise schools and teachers these days.

When I became a headteacher, much needed to be done in the school. We simply selected the most urgent things and attended to them. Nothing else was given any priority. As the situation changed, we moved on to the less important things, and then the minor ones.

We didn't write it all down. There wasn't any need. We knew exactly where we were going because we discussed it endlessly. After all, aren't heads, deputies and senior managers supposed to be appointed because they can see the wood for the trees? And doesn't the current practice of producing a mountain of paperwork take people away from actually getting things done?

A page in the document tells us to '*identify the school aim you will use to indicate current expectations. For example, it could be to ensure that all pupils achieve and make steady progress in their learning.*'

Can you really believe somebody would be daft enough to write that, and expect teachers not to howl with laughter? You can imagine how I felt about the other 89 pages. Come here, Grandma, I need to teach you how to suck eggs.

36

The greatest risk is that the teacher will go nuts

A friend of mine is a head of department in a secondary school. He is experienced, dedicated, an excellent teacher. RE isn't the easiest of subjects to teach, but children look forward to his lessons because he entertains them, and he continually seeks out new ways of capturing their interest and involving them. When he tells me about a lesson he's taught, I often think how much more enjoyable my own secondary school education would have been if I'd had a teacher like him.

But now a new broom is sweeping his academic corridors, and he's no longer a happy man. Before he teaches he has to fill in three sides of A4 paper. Not once a week, or even once a day. Before each and every lesson. I wondered why I hadn't seen him in his garden, and it seems he's kissed goodbye to evenings and weekends. The depth of planning he has to undertake is ludicrous, and virtually impossible to achieve without working every evening. Even Superman would have a struggle.

The lesson planning sheets are complex and detailed. On page one you fill in your name (get the tough ones over with first), the day, the date, the time of day, the room you're taking the lesson in, the class being taught and the topic you're teaching. Fortunately, you don't have to say what you've had for breakfast.

Then there's a space for your desirable outcomes. (To remain upright throughout the day, presumably?) Next, a slot for equipment requirements. (I shall need an overhead projector. I must remember to write down 'overhead projector' in case I forget. Oh, and some overhead trans-parencies. And pencils. And paper.)

Next, a section for 'key words', presumably important words and phrases you're trying to emphasise in the lesson. ('Andre, would you kindly stop firing screwed-up wet tissues at the ceiling' springs to mind.)

Now 'context' must be considered. There's quite a large space for that, whatever it is. Then we need to show how we're incorporating key skills, literacy, numeracy, ICT, citizenship and SMSC (sado-masochism for stressed colleagues?), all of which must be related to the lesson in hand and explained in a sentence or two.

Close behind are special needs, English as an additional language, hearing impairments and, of course, gifted and talented. Naturally, we need a full explanation of what these groups will be doing. Then, differentiated homework plans, and finally a risk assessment, just in case somebody is going to mix something in a test tube or put a drawing pin in the wall. As far as I can see, the greatest risk is that the teacher will go nuts and try to chew his own leg off.

But that's not it, yet. Not by a long chalk. Take a deep breath, because here comes page two! Now you have to sketch out your entire lesson structure for the three main elements: introduction, development and plenary. Not only the teacher's activity, mind, but a full explanation of what the children will be doing as well. Then there's a space for 'assessment oppor-tunities', 'lesson comments' and 'next week'. Presumably the latter is like a cinema trailer to whet the children's appetite for the next episode. ('Wow, I can hardly wait for next week! The chance to complete another photocopied worksheet because the poor bloody teacher's too busy to talk to us!')

And even now we haven't finished. Onwards, to the final page, where we find a 'class information sheet.' This time, we fill in the number on register, the number present, the able students (as opposed to disabled?), the classroom seating plan, the group ability, and the higher, middle, and lower ability students in the group.

Finally... do stay with it, we're almost there.. we have a space for any additional comments or suggestions. Well, I could think of a few. In fact, I'd suggest that whoever wrote the form should roll it up very tightly and.... But there, don't tempt me.

37

Babamide is interesting. He can drive a teacher insane...

Another summer over. Just when you're relaxed and used to treating the day as your own, education calls and you're into the autumn term. Groan.

But I don't groan very much. I look forward to seeing everybody again and autumn always brings renewed energy. And last year's new teachers are no longer 'newly qualifieds'.

Their voices have acquired that throaty tone of authority and they've emerged from their first year no longer viewing their charges as dewy-eyed innocents. They're ready to face them with that 'Come along young man, I wasn't trained yesterday' demeanour, revealing a teacher who has acquired a new confidence.

I was chatting to one of them yesterday, as she enthused about her new class. 'And just think,' I said, 'You haven't got Babamide this year.'

Babamide is the sort of child who can drive a teacher insane. Eight years old, stockily built and one of three children, none of whom is ever absent from school, he's a faithfully updated version of Richmal Crompton's William. Polite, earnest, friendly... and absolutely infuriating.

My mind wanders back to the last few weeks of summer term, when I'd find him working (I use the term very loosely) outside my room at least twice a week. I'd sigh, and the usual bizarre conversation would ensue.

'Hello, Babamide.'

'Hello Sir. I....'

'No, don't tell me, you've come to see me because you've been working especially hard.'

'No, my teacher sent me down here.'

'Really? For a sticker because you've done some good work?'

'No, because Nancy fell over on the stairs.'

'Don't tell me. You pushed her?'

'No, I was jus' walkin' like a chicken and she got in the way...'

'I see. You are aware that walking like a chicken is not our recommended method of travelling up the staircase?'

'Pardon?'

As usual, there's no point in pursuing the matter unless I want to be there until lunchtime, so I leave him, tongue enthusiastically emerging from the side of his mouth, struggling to draw the legs on a Roman soldier.

The next day, I'm listening to one of the violin groups, and I notice that Annisola, Babamide's sister, isn't using her own violin. Tentatively, I ask her where the violin is. I already know the answer.

'Babamide broke the string again. He keeps trying to play it.'

'Then why don't you hide it?'

'Me mum did. She put it on top of the wardrobe.'

'And he found it? How?'

'He sleeps on top of the wardrobe sometimes...'

Like all children, Babamide has lots of good points. He loves taking reading books home. The trouble is, he loses them. Three so far. He's been told he can't take more home until his father has paid for them. Worried about a walloping, he takes matters into his own hands and his teacher intercepts a letter to his dad, purportedly from her, that he's written himself. 'Dear Babamides Dad,' it says, 'I am pleesed to say Babamide as found his books so you won't hav to pay no munny.'

But time has moved on, and now his teacher has a new class. 'Funny thing is,' she says, 'I do rather miss him.'

She won't have too long to wait. His brother has just joined the Nursery.

94

38

'Am I a sardine?', asked Terry

Next time you visit my school, I'll let you have a look at my NOF certificate. What's that? Well, it's the certificate you get when you've successfully completed the rigorous government computer training course for teachers. I'm very proud of it, naturally.

Especially as I haven't done any of the training.

It all started when the government thought it would be a really good idea to make sure primary teachers knew how to integrate ICT across the curriculum. Forget that, at any given moment, schools are chasing their tails desperately trying to find money for keeping up with the constantly accelerating pace of technology, so quite a few of their computers are probably obsolete anyway.

Nevertheless, there was a big crock of government gold available for any firms who fancied running a little course for teachers, so they stepped forward in their hundreds. Some hadn't a clue, apart from knowing a quick buck when they saw one, but a handful survived, and I invited one of them to show me his wares.

I should have been warned when the laptop demo broke down twice, but the firm came highly recommended, we signed on the dotted line, and we duly assembled in our ICT room for the first session, accompanied by croissants and fresh coffee provided by our ICT co-ordinator, to bribe those who considered classroom computers an unreliable pain in the butt.

The first surprise was that the training would be via the internet. No fresh-faced, bright eyed young chappie guiding us through the jargon... just a handful of CDs and faceless mentors somewhere across the ether, gently forgiving every daft mistake.

I've been into computers since the days of BASIC and BBC Micros, so the second surprise was that the first two hours of this course were so boring even the croissants and coffee couldn't compensate. The e-mail system was incomprehensible, the electronic form-filling (that's all the course really consisted of) was deadly dull and the literature an unbeatable cure for insomnia.

Nevertheless, my wonderful staff, with the spirit that won us the war, slogged at it. I gave up at session two, simply turning up to smile at everybody else and fill up the tea urn.

And then, in session three, things turned interesting. We'd noticed that although everyone had an individual mentor, the feedback was remarkably similar. Identical, in fact. 'Well done Zoe, you are realising your learning and teaching objectives.' 'Well done Philip, you are realising your objectives for teaching and learning.'

By session four, we thought we'd test the water. So, in answer to: 'How did the children respond?' Terry wrote: 'By asking themselves basic questions like, 'am I a sardine?' And back came the response: 'Well done Terry, you are realising your objectives for teaching and learning.'

Was there a human across the ether, or were we being mentored by R2D2 and a sophisticated software program of stock responses?

Intrigued, Terry became bolder. 'What are your aims for the lesson?' the electronic form asked. 'For the children to have skills with the mouse, and for the mouse to have children skills,' he wrote. 'Well done Terry,' came the mentor's response, 'You are progressing well with your objectives for teaching and learning.'

By session six, and e-mails outlining how he'd found ICT lessons to be more successful when undertaken at the deep end of a swimming bath, somebody twigged and chastised him gently. He still got his certificate though. And, as I said, so did I.

But staff felt poorer for the experience, while the firm got a little bit richer. Still, we've all got our little bits of congratulatory paper, and the Government can assure itself it's putting us Luddite teachers right at technology's cutting edge.

39

She folded her arms and settled in for a long argument

When I was nine I took my atom bomb to school. It was an interesting bit of kit, consisting of a small metal ball sliced in two and held together by a hinge. You put a cap-gun pellet inside, swung it around on a string, and tossed it into the air. When it hit the ground the cap made a satisfying bang. Today's health and safety fanatics would have had a fit.

My friends were impressed, but my teacher wasn't. She held out her hand for the offending device, told me I knew toys shouldn't be brought to school, and said I could have it back at the end of term. I complained loudly to my mum. 'Serves you right,' she said. 'If you hadn't taken it to school you'd still have it now.' And that, as far as she was concerned, was that.

Cut to the 21st century, and the ubiquitous Beyblade. It's a sort of miniature spinning top, and for about six months, every boy had to have one. You wound a strap round it, pulled hard, and let it spin. You could have competitions with your mates, and they were even more fun at lunchtimes than having fights. Until, of course, somebody nicked one, which is what happened to Samuel.

I'd set out the Beyblade ground rules in assembly. As long as I saw them only in the playground, I'd be happy. For a while, the children stuck to the rules, and then the toys began appearing inside, mainly because they spun wonderfully on the stone staircases. Samuel had already been told three times not to play with his in the classroom, and in desperation his teacher took it from him, put it on her desk, and then forgot about it. When Samuel asked for it back, she realised it had disappeared.

She spent a lot of time trying to track the toy down. It didn't reappear, and the theft was discussed with Samuel's mother at an Open Evening. The teacher explained that even though we didn't condone the theft, the children had been told very clearly that they mustn't play with Beyblades inside the building. She also explained that she'd carried out an exhaustive search, it hadn't re-appeared, and unfortunately, given the circumstances, we couldn't take responsibility for the toy.

That, the teacher assumed, was the end of the matter. The next day, the secretary received a phone call from the mother. She wasn't satisfied. Didn't the teacher look after the things on her desk properly? How many other things went missing in her classroom? And what did the headteacher intend to do about the missing Beyblade? I got the feeling I was expected to go out straightaway and buy the boy a new one.

Eventually, the mother arrived at my door in person. Two of my teachers were off sick, a class was waiting for me, and the whistle was about to go. Nevertheless, I agreed to discuss the matter briefly.

She asked why the Beyblade hadn't been locked away safely in a drawer. I was astonished. The fact that Samuel shouldn't have been playing with the thing hadn't, it seemed, entered her reasoning. She folded her arms and settled in for a long argument. I pointed out that the discussion had finished and I had a class to go to, whereupon she strode off down the corridor, pausing only to ask the secretary how to make a formal complaint.

Soon the chair of governors was on the phone. The mother had been to the local authority offices and the complaints officer had passed the matter on to him. The parent was demanding an explanation, an apology, and a replacement, and the matter was elevated to an agenda item for the next governors' meeting.

With the education system creaking everywhere, it seemed very odd to me that we had a group of adults sitting around a table discussing Beyblades. Fortunately, when all the facts were known, common sense prevailed and the chair wrote a curt note to the parent. I banned Beyblades within a day.

My mother must have been gazing down in astonishment.

40

S for Selebrate...'

You probably aren't aware that I'm only 10 years old.

Okay, you've guessed. I'm not really, but the local authority sometimes treats me like a fluffy-brained youth. You see, I've just received a circular saying 'The council's vision for success is PRIDE in its education services.'

Well, okay, I'm proud of my school and quite a few other primary schools around me. I hope the council is too. But then the word PRIDE is repeated, and printed vertically, in great big letters, down the length of the page.

'P', it says, stands for 'promoting learning', 'R' for 'raising achievement', 'I' for 'instilling confidence', 'D' for 'developing competence', and 'E', would you believe, for 'empowering communities'. Great stuff. Magic. Thank you so much. We're all gratefully indebted to the fresh-faced council junior who concocted it.

Or, horror, was it put together by a team? Just imagine WPFACS (Working Party For Acrostics And Catchy Slogans) getting together to dream up this stuff...

'Gottit! What about EDUCATION? After all, that's the game we're in.'

'How do you spell EDUCATION?'

'OK then, something simpler. What about SOARING TO SUCCESS? S for Selebrate...'

'Too many S's. It needs to be catchy. What about ACCESS FOR ALL?'

'No, they'll think you're flogging a credit card. How about ACHIEV-ING EXCELLENCE?'

'Does the i come before the e? No, wait, there's a c in there, so wouldn't the e come before the i...'

'Simon, we haven't got all day. Let's go for a one-worder. PRIDE?'

'Wow, yes. Nice one Nigel. That'll give us Promoting, Raising, Instilling, Developing. What about the E? Education's too obvious. Energetic, Effective?'

'What about Empowering?'

'Empowering! Lovely word. Empowering what?'

'Children?'

'No no, broader, bigger!'

'Communities?'

'Super! What does it mean, empowering communities?'

'Nothing, really. Sounds *great* though. Five thousand copies before noon, Doris. Oh look, it's 10.30am already. Coffee break.'

And on it goes. Piles of paper. Mountains of nonsense. Money wasted that is desperately needed in schools. We're surrounded and bombarded by meaningless statements that presumably fooled some of the people some of the time, but can't be fooling any but the dewy-eyed these days.

All schools will tell you that a policy is needed for everything, because it keeps local officialdom, and inspectors in particular, very happy. It doesn't mean you have to do anything, you just need a policy. You don't even have to think one up, because several astute firms out there produce policies on CD databanks covering everything from Personal Health For Year 6 to Citizenship for the Under Fives. Just load 'em in the computer and put your school name where it leaves a space. Half an hour's work. And you've no idea how much it'll impress your governing body.

Meantime, when I drive to work, the streets are in poor repair and full of rubbish. I bet there's a policy for cleaning them up somewhere.

41

Anyway, who *is* Simon Rattle?

Morning, Donna. Did you have a good holiday?

Yes thank you, headmaster. The teachers aren't in yet. That's unusual, isn't it?

It would be normally, Donna. But not any more. From this term it's just you and the other teaching assistants.

So who's going to teach the children?

Dear, dear, you haven't been reading the newspapers. You see, the Government had a jolly good idea. Blue skies thinking, we call it. With the progress of technology, we don't need to waste money on all those expensive teachers; we just need one person in charge. Put the children in front of computer monitors, use people like you to watch over 'em, and our problem's solved.

But headmaster, the new ICT suite broke down four times last term.

I know, Donna. Sadly, we were ripped off by the firm that installed it. Still, we're not the only ones. Lots of other schools have been ripped off too.

Can't we get them in to sort things out?

They're not answering the phone. There's a message to say they're on holiday. In Bermuda. Still, mustn't complain. Some of our computers work. Sort of.

What about things like science experiments? I just don't have the knowledge...

You don't need it, Donna. The computer program deals with all that. The children watch the experiments on the monitor. Saves them messing about with test tubes. They only break the bloody things anyway.

But shouldn't children be experimenting with things?

Not these days. That sort of thinking went out with Plowden. And just think of the benefits. No health and safety rules, or hours spent writing risk assessments.

What about music, then? I can't even play a penny whistle.

Again, no problem Donna. The computer can simulate any instrument. Select cello, push a button, and you've got a cello. Easy to play, too. Just follow Mr Bouncy as he leads you through the Ode to Joy.

It's not real. And it doesn't sound it. People like Simon Rattle are concerned about music having low priority in primary schools. With all the other demands, teachers don't have enough time to do it.

Move into the 21st century, Donna. These days, kids download Mpegs and wavefiles. Learning a real instrument is far too time-consuming. Anyway, who's Simon Rattle?

What about English and maths? I can't teach them to SATS level.

You're not being asked to. There are thousands of worksheets you can use. Just print them from the computer and photocopy.

But worksheets are so boring.

Lots of things in life are boring, Donna.

The more I think about this, the more I worry. We don't have the expertise or discipline the teachers have. We couldn't possibly take them to concerts... or museums... or galleries.

How many more times, Donna. You won't need to. The computer will take you to the Tate and soon it'll all be in virtual reality anyway. Look at the savings on transport.

But the ethos of the school.. the friendships, the laughter. All the exciting events at Christmas.

Keep an eye on the ball, Donna. Our brief is to get the SATS results up, not run around playing Father Christmas..

Frankly, I think the Charlie who dreamed all this up is a complete idiot. Do you really want this for your own children, headmaster?

It won't affect me, Donna. My three are all at private school.

42

She'd march onto the roughest estate like John Wayne

The register lady visited yesterday. She's been around for years. I remember her from my own tender youth, though when I was in junior school she was a grey-haired gentleman called Mr Thistlewaite and he visited once a term, opened the register and called out a handful of names.

If he didn't hear a 'Yes, Sir' and he couldn't find a reason, he went knocking on the absentee's house that morning. I only tried truanting once. On the way to school, and a dreaded arithmetic test, I told my mum I felt sick. She looked at me sympathetically, and we walked back home. When I said I didn't feel sick enough to go to bed, I got a good clout, and I didn't miss any more school.

These days, I'm astonished at how easily children avoid school, and how much their parents pander to the slightest cough or whim.

'It's your birthday? Have the day off, son, and ask your friends too. We'll go to Thorpe Park.'

'Sorry Gavin wasn't in yesterday, but his hair needed cutting and we didn't want to waste any of the weekend.'

And then there are all the other events. OK, it's sad the rabbit died, but a week to get over the burial? Or the flight to Disneyland that George's parents booked during term time. 'I'm afraid he'll be off for two weeks, Could his teacher give him a little homework?'

But it's funny how, since SATS were invented, every child in Year 6 can turn up on time, every day, for the entire week of tests, because parents think they are desperately important.

During my first few years of headship, I was truly impressed by our register lady. In those days, she was called the attendance officer, and families soon knew that if you weren't in school and there wasn't a good reason, Tough Theresa would be banging on your door within the hour.

She was fearless, and would march on to the roughest estate like John Wayne routing the saloon bar baddies. Theresa visited us every week without fail, and she was as fit as an Olympic athlete. For a year or so, our attendance soared.

No more, though. These days the register lady is a key cog in the education welfare service and a major role is to check that teachers are filling in registers properly. This isn't as easy as it might sound, as the bewildering range of abbreviated codes and indicators makes it akin to picking up a Russian primer for the first time.

Now, I appreciate that filling in registers is important, particularly as they could be used in court, but checking us so regularly seems a little excessive. And it's not just my school, of course, but every other school in the local authority, so quite a few hours of truant-catching time is being used up. And when a child has taken lots of time off school, there's the usual welter of form-filling to be done, often for a result that makes you wonder if it was worth the effort.

Take Darren, for example. He's six, already beyond his mum's control, and long since separated from his absentee dad. Mum wants him to go to school, and most days she gets him there, though usually very late. In school, he's fine. He's able and works hard, and he appreciates the clear boundaries. At home, there aren't any boundaries, because his mum is unable to create any.

If Darren wants to stay up half the night, he does. And then he'll sleep in, of course. The best the welfare service can come up with is to suggest Darren attends 'anger management' courses. And as Darren does actually get to school most days, he's a low welfare priority.

Soon, he'll truant. In the meantime, let's make sure we're all using the right ink in our registers.

43

I couldn't believe how tedious his assemblies were

Headship is a funny thing. You're the lord of your manor, with control over everything that happens in it. It's an awesome responsibility and needs to be thought about often, lest you fall into the trap of thinking you're omnipotent, and that way disaster lies.

I've known many headteachers in my career; some I've admired, some I've had lively debates with, and the behaviour of a few has ranged from mildly eccentric to... well, giving extreme cause for concern. I've worked for a couple in the latter group.

The first was a very dull gentleman. People fell asleep in his staff meetings. As a young, enthusiastic teacher, I couldn't believe how tedious his assemblies were. We'd file into the hall, and Mrs Simpson would thunder out 'All Things Bright and Beautiful', the efficacy of her playing depending on whether the string holding the pedals together survived her energetic footwork.

Then we'd have the Lord's Prayer, a telling-off because a school rule had been broken, and out we'd go again. It was an utterly pointless 20 minutes. Thinking about it now, perhaps it was the Lord's way of saying: 'Kent, when you achieve headship, never, ever, do an assembly like this.'

His limited teaching career can't have been inspiring, either; if teachers were ill and he was forced to take a class, he'd always do exactly the same lesson – graphs illustrating the children's favourite animals, colours, football teams, or anything. Once, when we were desperately short-staffed and I was due at a swimming gala, he offered to teach my children, asking if there was anything particular I'd like him to do. 'You could draw some graphs of their favourite outings,' I suggested. 'Good idea!' he said.

The second head had a thing about lost property. Brought up in an age of greater austerity, he expected children to label their clothing and belongings and keep track of them at all times. Occasionally, he'd find a single plimsoll or glove in the corridor, and in assembly the children would be told to check whether they were in possession of a full set of limbs, because he failed to see how any idiot could walk around with only one shoe on.

By half term, the lost property pile had grown relentlessly and he'd bring it into assembly, holding each piece at arm's length like an overripe kipper. Nobody would claim anything, of course, and when really upset he'd been known to toss much of it out of his office window, where it adorned the branches of a tree in the playground until the premises officer removed it with a skilfully aimed rake.

But these two paled beside the head a friend worked for. He disliked children and spent much of his time avoiding them – which wasn't difficult because his room was in the bowels of the building, adjacent to his en-suite washroom. His school life was divided between meetings and riding his horse on Hampstead Heath.

On a fine day he would frequently come to assembly clad in jodhpurs and riding jacket, and the staff knew there would be no point in trying to find him that afternoon. Apart from his horse, his greatest pleasure was his massive deputy, with whom he was having a relationship, and occasionally they'd duet in assembly, she on the piano, him singing.

On the first occasion, children and staff were stunned into disbelieving silence, which the couple took to be appreciation. This rapidly waned when the concerts increased in frequency, until, one morning, the performance was halted and the head rose to his full 5ft 2in.

'Your attention span is on a par with a tin of maggots,' he roared at the children. Then he stormed out of the hall.

I often wonder what Ofsted would have made of him.

44

I arrive at school to be told there isn't a job after all

It's September and I've got three new teachers, all newly qualified. Their enthusiasm is infectious, and as I chat with them my mind leaps back 40 years to my very first week in the classroom.

If you wanted to work in London in those days, you picked an area you fancied and applied to its education office, which simply allocated you to a school with a vacancy. I chose Islington, a pretty grim place at that time.

Monday

I arrive at my school to be told there isn't a job after all. The local authority has made a mistake, but if I wait in the staffroom the head will sort things out. By 11.30, I'm still there. The secretary says sorry, it's the first day of term and things are busy, but if I go back to the staffroom the head will phone the office right now.

By lunchtime, the LEA lines are still busy. He'll try this afternoon. I remain in the staffroom, looking keen and reading a book on educational philosophy. People passing through the room smile cautiously, wondering who I am. By home time, I've finished the book and think it might be worthwhile starting *War and Peace*.

Tuesday

The head hasn't talked with the education office, but that's not surprising, he says, because it's often three days into the new term before telephone contact can be made. However, Class 4 is going to the Tower of London this morning, and help would be appreciated, so would I like to go?

When we arrive, I'm allocated six children, none of whom behaves particularly well, and when we return to school I feel like an exhausted tourist. The head approaches as I devour a hasty sandwich. Would I mind going back to the Tower this afternoon? It's just that Class 3 is going and Mrs Smith likes help with the difficult ones on outings. I have the feeling it's not an offer I'm allowed to refuse.

My group includes Andrew, who darts off every few minutes, desperate to spend the small amount of money his auntie has given him. When we return, Andrew's satchel bulges suspiciously with the vast number of artefacts he says he 'bought'. I sleep restlessly that night.

Wednesday

The head has spoken to the LEA, but there are no vacancies at other local schools yet. I'm to wait in the staffroom while he finds me something to do. I've forgotten my book, so I complete the crossword in a tatty Woman's Own.

An elderly teacher nips in for a quick smoke. Her Year 6 class is across the corridor, she tells me, and they won't miss her for 10 minutes. She asks why I chose this career, and says she can't wait to finish hers. She doesn't like the head; far too young, and he favours all this fashionable topic-based nonsense.

Indignantly, she sniffs and tells me how he threw away all her history books. 'Had 'em 30 years and I bloody well wasn't having that, so my children climbed in the bins and fetched 'em out again.'

I make a discreet exit, and meet the head in the corridor. He sends me to the dinner hall to help out. I stand about like a wet lettuce, not understanding the rites and rituals of dinner duty. A child drips semolina onto my suedes.

Thursday

The head has been sent some more visitor vouchers for the Tower of London. Class 2 is going this morning, so it would be very useful if I went along. And Class 7 will be going this afternoon. Could I help with them too? I look on the bright side. After all, I'm learning a hell of a lot about ravens.

Friday

The head talks to the education office, and they still don't know what to do with me. Could the school keep me, and they'll foot the bill for the extra teacher? The deputy head feels sorry for me and suggests I have her class, while she becomes non-teaching. I'm very excited as I hurry to meet the children and explain all the interesting things I'm going to do with them.

Which won't include visiting the Tower of London.

45

'Oh, wow... the rabbit's laid an *egg*, Miss!'

There's something very special about working with the under fives in the Nursery class. Do it well, like my inspiring Nursery teacher, and you give small children a thirst and passion for learning which can last a lifetime. Mess it up, and you create a wet playtime situation where children simply become bored and distressed.

As I go in on my daily visit, they're sitting in a circle singing a song about Sandy, who's lonely and wants a friend to dance with on the beach. Senna's in the ring, and she picks Alfie, who jumps up and grabs her with gusto. They cavort happily, until the verse finishes and it's Alfie's turn to choose. You'd never believe it, but it's only a couple of months since Alfie showed an unpleasant tendency to whack his teacher in the stomach and jump on the backs of his peers. Looking at him now, he's almost eligible for *Come Dancing*.

The children disperse for their activities, and Hana and Sadie ask if I'd like my hair done. Without waiting for an answer, they lead me to their corner 'salon', ask me to pick a style, then assault my head with brushes, curlers and pins. I pray that my dandruff shampoo has done its work. I'm tidied up and told to look in the mirror. The children chuckle as I move on, curlers still in my hair.

I sit down with the twins, Ron and Ed, who joined us recently. Mum is very proud of 'her boys', but so, I recall, was Mrs Kray. Ron and Ed are constructing a building from wooden blocks. It falls, pieces narrowly missing two children on the carpet. I suggest they shouldn't make the next one so tall, and we explore ways of making a firmer base. Ed flicks a block into my lap, then stares at me. 'What are you gonna do about that?' his eyes ask. I move on.

Shadna started today. Quiet, shy and with little English, she watches everything that's going on. I smile at her and tell her what a beautiful dress she has on. 'I wish I had a beautiful dress like that,' I say. She looks at me in disbelief and bursts into a fit of giggles. Sultana, the nursery assistant, takes her gently by the hand to see the guinea pigs. Her brother was fascinated by the guinea pigs, and his language rapidly improved because he wanted to talk about them.

Ellie and Julie are exploring water, a wonderful activity when you're small. Their sleeves rolled up, they experiment with a range of containers. They live next door to each other in a high-rise block and, as they pour, they chat. 'Fat Darren ain't with us no more,' says Ellie.

'Ain't 'e?' replies Julie, interested.

'No,' says Ellie. 'Me mum chucked 'im out. Fed up with 'im. 'E didn't 'alf go a wallop.' A story there, I think, but I decide not to ask.

'Come and see what we've found,' says Hamid, grabbing my hand and urging me to the garden area where his friends are poring over the earth they've been churning. 'We've got worms.' I admire the juicy pair they've discovered, and we discuss how they feed.

'Can't see how they do that,' says George. 'They ain't got no face.' They decide to take them inside for a closer look under the microscope. I keep my fingers crossed for the worms.

If Ofsted's hackneyed phrase 'awe and wonder' belongs anywhere, it has to be with the under-fives. Recently, Lucy and Sharleen were startled by a new arrival in the rabbit's hutch.

'Oh, wow! Look, an egg, the rabbit's laid an *egg* Miss!' cried Lucy, pointing at the round white shape newly nestled among the straw in the box. She was so excited the teacher hadn't the heart to tell her one of the children had thought the rabbit might like something to play with, and had popped a table tennis ball in the hutch...

46

By the time I'd heard the last option I'd forgotten the first one

I'd spent a pleasant half-hour before school setting up the new printer for the library computer, and I just had to load the driver.

Simple. We'd be up and running in minutes. I hunted for the usual CD but for some reason it wasn't in the packaging. Irritated, I phoned the company we'd bought it from, to be told they didn't carry spare driver CDs. They'd have to send a whole new kit, but there was a three-week wait. Sorry.

Never mind. The morning was young. I could phone the manufacturer and ask for a driver to be posted. A recorded voice thanked me for ringing, and please would I listen to the following list of options. By the time I'd heard the last one I'd forgotten the number of the option I needed.

I dialled again, selecting the one that offered me a human being. A voice told me that all the operatives were busy, but someone would answer just as soon as possible, so don't go off and take assembly because the waiting time would simply fly by and here's an electronic version of the 'Eine Kleine' for your delectation.

Eventually, a soft Scottish brogue (why do these huge American corporations always have call centres in Scotland?) announced that she was Karen and she'd like to be of assistance to me. I told Karen I was really happy about that because I needed a driver for my Hi-Whizzo Ten-Ink Pro-Zoom multi-tasking printer.

Karen wasn't too sure what a driver was, but she was certain the service department could help, so she'd transfer me immediately. I hoped I wouldn't have to listen to the 'Eine Kleine' played on an eight-note digital keypad again. She assured me I wouldn't.

Seconds later Mozart returned, interrupted by a voice saying unfortunately all our operatives are busy but someone will be with you just as soon as possible so whatever you do don't hang up. I looked at my watch. I was in danger of missing assembly altogether, but having got this far I couldn't bear starting again.

Eventually, Mozart was interrupted and Hamish said he'd like to be of assistance. That's good, I said, because I'm having a little problem with my Hi-Whizzo printer. Before he could 'process my request', Hamish said he'd need the serial and model numbers. Then he'd give me a job reference I could quote if I needed to call again. I said that if all calls took as long as this, rigor mortis might have set in by the time he phoned again, so could he hang on while I nipped to the library for the information? Yes, Hamish would gladly hang on.

Naturally, the numbers he wanted were stamped in an obscure place on the bottom of the machine, but he was still then when I picked up the phone again. Now all I needed was the CD with the printer driver. 'Ah, sorry,' said Hamish, 'we don't carry those. But I could give you the number of the company that handles them for us.'

This time I got a butchered Brandenburg Concerto, and Eleanor, who wanted to know how she could help me. Did she, perchance, stock printer drivers? Yes, she did. And did she stock one for the Hi-Whizzo Ten-Ink Pro-Zoom Multi-tasker? Yes, she did. My elation knew no bounds.

Could she then – I trembled inwardly – post me one? She could, and if I held the line she'd check her stock. Butchered Brandenburg resurfaced, and so did Eleanor, to tell me she had drivers for every printer from the entry level Idiotjet right up to the HokeyCokey 3000, but not one for the Hi-Whizzo. It was a very new printer and they were waiting for the drivers to arrive. Sorry. Had I tried the company that sold me the printer in the first place? A tear dribbled down my cheek as I went off to assembly.

I did get the driver in the end, though. I downloaded it from the internet.

It only took me a week.

47

If it swung back, it would remove all his teeth

During one of our Ofsted inspections, a teacher performed a simple experiment to show how much oxygen there is in air. It involved placing a jam jar over a lighted candle. The inspector asked for the risk assessment sheets, and the teacher chuckled at this tension-breaking flash of humour. But no, this wasn't a joke – she was really expected to have written out a full risk assessment simply because she was sticking a jar over a lighted candle.

I sometimes feel we're roaming around in ever-decreasing circles of insanity. We see horrifying violence all around us and yet we molly-coddle children in school to the point where we're even beginning to wonder if playtimes are a good idea. After all, there's usually only one teacher on duty, and if Charlie has an accident then Mrs Brown may well rub her hands at the prospect of compensation.

There's certainly no shortage of health and safety 'specialists' eager to tell you what you're doing wrong. At a price. Fortunately, the person who visited us recently was paid by the authority, not me. The computers were too high, the stools too low, the room too light, the furniture too cramped, the electric cable too visible. And that was just the ICT room. I'm glad she didn't look in the PE cupboard.

Every now and then schools are alerted to a new health issue. Cabin hooks, for example, which keep connecting doors open. A while ago an urgent directive was issued to premises officers telling them to remove these hooks from the doors along corridors and at entrances to halls. The thinkers and planners had decided that if a fire broke out and the doors in the school were hooked back, the flames would spread more rapidly. I refused to remove them, and I had my reasons carefully prepared when the fire officer arrived.

I explained that in 40 years of teaching in buildings like this one, I'd never seen a fire, and that, if there was no adult in sight, children would sprint through the doors on their way out to play Spider-man (health and safety unapproved version) because children were children. Then I stood an infant in front of a door, showing how, if it slapped back, the doorknob would effectively remove all his teeth. In my view, the danger of a fire was therefore considerably lower than the likelihood of a door-knobbed face. The officer nodded gravely, jotted down a note or two, and left. I didn't hear from him again.

We spend so much time thinking about health and safety nowadays that children are in danger of missing out on many enjoyable activities. A farm visit, Kate? Great idea! I'm sure your Reception class would love it, but what about the food poisoning organisms present in farm animals? Campylobacter, salmonella, cryptosporidium, that sort of thing.

What about the suitability of places the children can eat? What about their footwear, the risk of infection from animal bedding, the dangers of foodstuff and animal faeces, the importance of remembering to dress cuts and grazes appropriately and ensure little hands are washed? And since small children have a tendency to kiss the animals, better warn them about that too...

Then there's the whole debate about whether children should visit farms at all. It's a far cry from the days when I took children on two-week school trips to the Isle of Wight, where we always spent a day on a farm, often having a go on the tractor as well...

Yes, we're wary these days to the point where useful and enjoyable learning activities are being thrown out with the bathwater, though when one of my teachers wanted his class to build miniature balsa wood coffins for their Egyptian mummies and asked if we had any Stanley knives and glue guns, I nearly had a fit.

48

Can I borrow you and your JCB?

The other day I heard that another school had dispensed with its premises officer. The head had decided to employ someone to lock and unlock the building, and then buy in other services only when they were needed.

I suppose it's a way of saving some money, but it's a growing trend that surprises me, because a good premises officer is as crucial to a school's success as an able secretary, or administration officer as they're known these days. If the premises officer lives on site, especially with a large dog, vandalism is cut to a minimum, but there's a lot more to it than that.

Our premises officer hasn't been with us long, but he'd done occasional days for us and I was keen to appoint him when the incumbent officer retired. He took over at an awful time. We were being rewired, and up to the last week of the summer holiday there were bits of broken plaster and brick everywhere. Not only did Dave manage to get everything spotless for the beginning of term, he was always available to help teachers rearrange and organise their classroom furniture. He was genuinely touched when they had a collection for him, though they'd been equally surprised to find a schoolkeeper with such endless cheerfulness and enthusiasm.

An avid Millwall supporter, he was soon running football teams after school and entering them into local tournaments. Before long, we'd filled a shelf outside my room with pots and shields. He's also shown himself to be a man who can turn his hand to most DIY jobs, and if he can't do it, he'll know someone who can. When my Mini suffered a puncture and I'd left my jack at home, I could hear Dave dragging the hefty jack he'd borrowed from the car wrecker's yard five streets away.

But his greatest talent is grabbing an opportunity when he sees one. We'd decided to get rid of the old, disused outside lavatories to create an environmental area, and Dave got a quote from the local education authority. Taken aback by the suggested £6,000, he said he'd 'have a little think about it'. A fortnight later I drove into school to find a heap of rubble where the toilets had been. For a moment I thought he'd attacked them with a sledgehammer. But no, it seemed he'd spotted a man driving a JCB along the road, walked out and offered £200 cash if he'd drive his digger straight into the lavs. The man obliged and the children in Year 6 spent many happy playtimes tossing broken bricks into a skip while Dave saved the good ones for building the flower beds.

Which was how we discovered his wife had a talent too. For someone brought up in the city, she has the greenest fingers imaginable. If she planted a stick in the ground and watered it, it would grow. Like Dave, Debbie has an eye for a bargain, and to fill the new flower beds she visited the local market, made friends with the traders and charmed them into delivering huge quantities of plants and shrubs at ridiculously low prices.

That Spring, our playground looked a treat: hanging baskets, beds and tubs, small trees in neat brick beds and clematis-covered fencing everywhere. Two gardening clubs were started to maintain this floral abundance. And still the plants arrived, so Debbie bought lots of baskets and made them into Mother's Day gifts for the children at pocket money prices. Soon, the wall of football trophies was supplemented by certificates and awards from City in Bloom competitions.

It seems to me that any school not cultivating the talents of its premises officer is missing out. Chatting to Dave after a governors' meeting one night, I commented on the length of his working day. 'Yes, it is long,' he agreed, 'but I've never been happier.'

Looking at what he and his wife have added to our school, the feeling is mutual.

49

Oh no, it's a Powerpoint Presentation

This morning, I'm going to talk to you about achievable targets. This morning, I'm going to talk to you about achievable targets.

It won't have escaped your notice that I said that twice. Why? Because I'm doing a PowerPoint presentation.

I saw my first PowerPoint presentation years ago, when the local education authority invited its headteachers to discuss its latest initiative. Instead of the ubiquitous overhead projector and transparencies, a large electronic whiteboard hung impressively on the wall, connected to a laptop and a device that looked like a slide projector.

For a moment I wondered if we were about to enjoy the chief inspector and his wife on Brighton beach in glorious widescreen, but no, this was a talk about setting achievable targets. Well, it would be, wouldn't it. But this was a lot more entertaining than the average LEA meeting.

Each time the speaker made what he thought was an important point, he'd push a button and the sentence he'd just said would animate its letters across the whiteboard and then underline itself. Was this new whizzo presentation of wise words intended for ageing heads who tend to nod off as soon as somebody other than themselves starts talking? No, it was simply a new piece of flashy technology, and it was there to impress. After the talk, I investigated the cost. For the same price, I could have bought 212 guitars for my school. Or 72 overhead projectors. Still, at least it didn't go wrong.

Today's laptops and software programs can do wondrous things, but, because they're more complicated, they foul up more often. I remember the sales rep who wanted to earn our custom for a government-funded training scheme. He opened his laptop and had barely got two minutes into his demo before a failing battery caused the machine to stumble to a halt.

He was certain he had a spare battery with him, but after rummaging through his case, his pockets, and every inch of his BMW, he realised he'd lost the sale.

Of course, Sod's law states that the reliability of a piece of technology is in inverse proportion to the size and importance of the audience watching you use it, and the law was certainly in operation on a recent course I attended. Groups of heads were talking about raising achievement for boys, and all the groups except two were using PowerPoint presentations, though I'm certain their talks weren't that much better for it. They just looked prettier.

Halfway through the afternoon, one of the laptops crashed, and the embarrassed female headteacher stared at it in bewilderment. Male technophiles quickly leapt to her rescue, and for ten minutes bodies were bent over the apparatus while plugs were pushed and pulled, cables substituted and buttons pressed.

Confronted from my front row seat by a line of bums, I peered up at the screen, which, almost gleefully I felt, kept displaying those annoying little Windows messages saying it couldn't make any sense of the input. In the end, the woman was forced to improvise her talk, and I felt enormous sympathy for her. I bet she does her next presentation with a piece of paper.

But the technophiles won the day, of course. One headteacher proudly gave a PowerPoint presentation that amounted to a set of visual fireworks. Animated characters jumped and jiggled on the screen, words and sentences exploded in dazzling colour. It was so eye-popping I still haven't a clue what his talk was actually about.

It must have taken weeks to prepare. I couldn't help wondering whether his time might have been more profitably spent listening to children read.

50

Caroline turned up in what looked like carpet slippers

School Administration Officers are crucial to the success of a school. Appoint a bad one and they can cock everything up with alarming speed.

Doreen was retiring. She'd served us very well for many years and we needed to appoint a replacement. Fortunately, we had the ideal person to hand. Sandra was a teaching support assistant, adept with any age group. She had the right qualifications, excellent relationships with everyone and was efficient with parents and paperwork. She also had a delightful sense of humour and was very keen to do the job. What more could you ask?

At the next governors' meeting, I suggested we wouldn't find a better person, and that we should appoint her. Everybody agreed except Anthony, who doesn't come to many meetings, and when he does, he's late. He's on the personnel committee, and he said it was important that we followed the rules by advertising and interviewing. Other governors nodded, so we discussed dates for the committee to meet. Unfortunately, Anthony couldn't make any of them, but he said it was fine for us to go ahead without him.

We spent an evening drawing up an eye-catching advertisement, and I phoned the local paper to see how much a couple of insertions would cost.

Horrified at the price, I reduced it to one, which was fortunate, because the phone didn't stop ringing for two weeks after it appeared. I asked Anthony if he'd like to help me draw up a job description, but unfortunately he was busy that day.

By the end of the week I'd printed, packaged, posted or e-mailed 73 application forms and detailed job descriptions. It took a great deal of time to go through the applications and give them the attention they deserved. I'd asked Anthony to help, but unfortunately he was busy, so I divided them between the remaining three of us on the personnel committee.

Some were weeded out quickly; two years as a swimming pool attendant was not quite the experience I was looking for, and a spell as a bookie's assistant didn't really light my fire. But eventually I shortlisted half a dozen from my pile. Then it was back to the other committee members to see what they'd come up with. I didn't get much school work done that week.

Ten applicants (more postage, stamps, phone calls) were invited in to look around the school. It's always fascinating to compare the reality with what's written on an application form. I hadn't bargained for Caroline turning up in what looked suspiciously like carpet slippers, and Deirdre may have been nervous, but after half an hour of being unable to get a word in edgeways I felt I'd been verbally ravaged.

By the time I'd shown the last person round the school I'd forgotten what the first one looked like, but after another long evening with the personnel committee we managed to whittle the number of applicants down to five people. Plus Sandra.

On to the interview, and by now my wife was getting used to the idea of eating alone. I'd hoped Anthony would be available for the interviewing panel, but unfortunately he was very busy that week. On a rainy evening, all the candidates turned up in their Sunday best, ready to convince us that salary was the last thing on their minds, because they all knew how cash-strapped schools were. All six smiled a great deal and said how wonderful they thought children were. Particularly Sandra.

By 10.30 that night, it was all over. What did the committee decide? Yes, we appointed Sandra.

I didn't even bother telling Anthony...

51

I was turning green and couldn't be responsible for my actions

During assembly, Dipak broke wind, causing great merriment among the children around him. I told him to leave the hall immediately, and later I pointed out severely that if he did it again he and I wouldn't be the best of chums.

No doubt if I'd discussed my reaction with a behaviour therapist I'd have been told I'd got it all wrong. Dipak should have been given an in-depth session with the educational psychologist. Or offered fart management. Then again, perhaps it was my fault. My assembly might have been so boring he needed to distract himself by breaking wind. Or what about a group therapy session, where he could shed his torment and remove the angst from his system?

In fact, I did none of those things. I told him off, because he was being naughty. Strange as it might seem, children sometimes are, but a massive industry has grown around the pretence that children are really adults, only smaller, and that there is a psychological reason for every bit of naughtiness. Teachers are caught in the middle, hardly daring to tell Charlie off because he might have a huge personal file and a syndrome that starts with 'dys'. While some kind of solution is being devised, little Charlie is being a constant pain in the butt during lessons.

After years of dealing with every kind of behaviour problem, I still find the unorthodox method often works best. Take Freddie. A place suddenly became available in Year 5, and Freddie was at the top of the waiting list. I invited him and his mother to look around the school. He chatted politely and, as we wandered round, Mum explained that he'd been badly bullied at his current school. He'd been in a lot of fights, she said, although it was never his fault. Then she mentioned that he was attending anger management therapy on Sunday mornings.

Warning bells rang, and as soon as they'd gone I phoned his school. There was a sigh of relief that he might be moving, and the deputy explained that she'd had innumerable meetings with Mum about his temper. Other parents had complained endlessly.

Never one to resist a challenge, I decided to accept him, and on his first morning I outlined my general philosophy about our school. 'This is a great place to be,' I said, 'with all sorts of things to get into. But you have to be friendly and tolerant towards everybody else. That's the only rule. I don't want the Incredible Hulk here.' He nodded enthusiastically.

Within two days he was in a fight at playtime. I spoke to him again. Within a week he was in another, and ordered to my room. When he'd cooled down, I asked him to walk down to lunch with me. As we reached the staircase I suddenly raised my voice in great pain, thrust my chest out, roared loudly, flailed my arms, and threw my coat to the floor, shouting to Freddie to stand well back as I was turning green and couldn't be responsible for my actions. For a minute he looked absolutely terrified, and then he grinned broadly as he realised I was acting.

'You see,' I said, 'I've just managed my anger. Now you manage yours, or you're out. OK?'

We've got on well since then, although Sandra the secretary had heard my Hulk impression with much concern. 'I thought you'd finally flipped,' she said. Perhaps I have, but there are times when a little eccentricity goes a long way. And Freddie smiles much more these days.

52

Lennie was destined to be a plumber

So far, I haven't put a sign up in the playground saying, 'No parents past this point', but sometimes I'm sorely tempted.

It's easy to forget that most parents are more than happy with what we provide, because, increasingly, my time is taken up with those who over-indulge their children. Often, they refuse to believe their offspring could possibly do or say anything wrong, even in the face of irrefutable evidence.

Take Braidon, for instance. Not an easy boy by any stretch of the imagination, with a considerable talent for causing problems in the playground and then moving well away to avoid shouldering any blame when a teacher arrives on the scene. Because he was intelligent, we managed to steer him into positive activities most of the time.

But I remember the morning when a local sweetshop owner came to see me, distraught at Braidon's behaviour. Braidon had been caught stealing and asked to leave, whereupon he spent the next half an hour throwing snowballs into the shop, smothering customers and stock with snow and mud. I offered to phone his mother, who curtly said she'd look into the matter. Shortly afterwards, I heard that she'd charged into the shop, hurling abuse at the shopkeeper and saying her son wouldn't do anything like that. Braidon stood behind her, grinning.

You wouldn't think it, but even a relatively minor offence such as being late for school is ripe for a challenge. Alex's mum came to see me, waving the letter I'd just sent her saying Alex was late for school far too often.

She took a very dim view of letters like that, she said. After all, didn't statistics show that children who were late for school were more successful in later life than those who weren't?

I pointed out that whatever the statistics said, it was her legal duty to ensure Alex came to school when he was supposed to. Unimpressed, she strode off down the corridor. I didn't have time to voice my other concern: the six-inch kitchen knife she'd packed in Alex's lunch box for peeling his orange.

But at least Alex didn't damage school property. Lennie did. Lennie was a Year 1 infant who was destined to be a plumber, though unfortunately he spent a great deal of his time dismantling things rather than putting them together.

Sink drainage systems would suddenly leak in the washrooms, toilet seats would be unbolted on one side causing the occupant to swerve wildly, and door locks would be fiddled with, even though the firm who fitted them had assured us they were tamper-proof. Lennie, it seemed, could unscrew the inscrutable.

Then, while removing the chains from the playground lavatories, he pulled one too hard, causing the cistern to break away from the wall. His father, when summoned, inspected the damage sniffily. 'Oh well,' he said. 'Boys will be boys.' When it was suggested that he might make a contribution towards repairs, or at least stop Lennie's pocket money, he was astonished. 'What on earth do we pay our rates for?' he said.

All this pales beside the comment made by a former editor of a national newspaper, in one of the lucrative columns he writes. After stating that school nativity plays are often tedious little affairs, he quotes with pride his own son's comment when coerced into playing a shepherd.

'Oh shut up, you freaks!' the boy shouted on stage to the cast. 'Now *that*,' said his father, 'is what I call a star!'

If that's to be admired, is it any wonder that teachers spend so much of their time battling the current yob culture?

53

Stuff like this takes educational garbage to a new level

One picture is worth a thousand words, as the saying goes. If you've ever tried to assemble a piece of flat-packed furniture, you'll undoubtedly agree.

On the other hand, my staff and I recently sat through a training video that defies belief. It was forty five minutes long and as logical as Alice in Wonderland. It was also excruciatingly, staggeringly, mind-numbingly boring. I simply cannot believe that professionals are meant to take it seriously. Stuff like this, said a colleague, takes educational garbage to a new level.

Are doctors required to watch a video telling them it's a good idea to ask a patient how he's feeling before attempting a diagnosis? Are dentists told that before they can start any work, it's sensible to get the patient to open his mouth?

I know I complain about much of the documentation that emanates from our educational lords and masters and I suspect it's the same in all professions these days, but I'm still passionately interested in education and I do try to keep up with it all.

When this package arrived I tried, as always, to look on the positive side. '*Excellence and Enjoyment!*' shouted the headline from the glossy booklet. '*Continuing Professional Development*' declared the beautiful white lettering on the video, above a photo of three immaculately dressed women (who obviously hadn't been near the paintpots and papier mache recently) poring over a laptop and no doubt still at school at 7pm busily setting new targets for driving up standards.

As I thumbed through the booklet (and remember, this costly package had been sent to every primary school in the country), I couldn't believe the nonsense I was reading. One of the principles underlying teaching young children, we are told, is 'the use of assessment to help learners improve their work'. Really? Gosh. And I wouldn't mind betting that one of the prime requisites for a brickie is a bit of cement to stick the bricks together.

I read further. As a teacher, I'm told, I should 'set high expectations' and 'establish what learners already know'. Then (wait for it...) I can build on it.'

Dear God, have our young teachers spent three years training without being told these illuminating basics? More to the point, are teachers so daft they can't work out this sort of thing for themselves? And that's just the booklet. When you get to the video, things get even worse. I played it at a staff meeting.

Now, I have a dedicated and enthusiastic team of teachers, open to new ideas and techniques, but they're unwilling to suffer fools gladly. For the first five minutes they dutifully watched the video, while I watched their faces. Soon, they began to glance at each other; then the smiles appeared. After 10 minutes everyone was laughing uproariously, because even though the people on the video were talking non-stop, none of us had the slightest idea what they were trying to tell us. Where, I wondered, does the Department for Education find people like this? Do you have to win some sort of silliness contest?

The worthy ladies on screen sat wittering away about structure and scaffolding and whole-staff reflection and scrutiny and systems of trialling (whatever they are), and none of them seemed to be hearing each other in any meaningful way. Samuel Beckett would have loved it. After fifteen minutes we turned it off and talked instead about ways to improve children's handwriting.

Nevertheless, it worries me that schools put up with this expensive and unnecessary claptrap. It lands in staffrooms and teachers either don't look at it, or they watch it, decide it doesn't have the slightest bearing on any kind of educational reality and then dump it in Pseud's Corner where it rightly belongs.

In future, though, perhaps we shouldn't do that. I'm sending my package back, with a strong letter saying what we thought of it. And if even 10 per cent of the 26,000 schools who receive this rubbish on a regular basis do the same thing, perhaps we can batter a little sense into the suited dullards who think this is really what we need in our staffrooms.

54

If you want all them balloons blown up, pass 'em to the mothers

Celebrities and school aren't an ideal mix. Returning from an educational outing recently, Class 3 spotted a TV actress through the coach window. The following day their accounts of the trip contained little about the visit, but a great deal about living and loving in *Coronation Street*.

And when Year 6 took part in a children's TV quiz programme, they returned to school so elated from hurling custard pies at each other their teachers spent days coaxing them into picking up a pencil.

Which is why I was in two minds when our local MP asked if Gordon Brown could visit and chat to the parents, hopefully fired by election fever, outside the school gate. I eventually agreed, as we'd been talking to the children about elections and how they work. And if I could get close enough to Gordon, I could ask him for a blank cheque to finish my school garden...

Our MP also asked if I'd mention the Chancellor's visit to parents, and since I was finishing a newsletter, I suggested I put it in that. 'Good idea,' she said. Within three minutes she was back on the phone saying that, actually, it wasn't such a great idea after all. Half the neighbourhood might descend, and there would be all kinds of security problems.

Then a call came from Labour's Central Office, asking for a resume of the school by e-mail so that Gordon could be briefed before arriving. I hurriedly typed a short note, saying what an utterly wonderful school we are, but we wouldn't mind an extra fiver or so to finish the school garden.

Friday dawned, and by 8am photographers had commandeered the road outside the gates. Labour party aides arrived soon afterwards, several asking if they could pop into the school powder room. I agreed, warning them that our powder room might not meet the health and safety standards they were accustomed to at party headquarters.

Then, as parents and children began to wander inquisitively towards the school gates, boxes of leaflets and stickers were unpacked, and bright red balloons distributed. My little group of 'challenging' mothers, always ready to grumble about anything to do with school, perched themselves on the low wall opposite, inspecting the scene suspiciously. 'If you want all them balloons blown up,' advised one of their husbands, nodding towards the group, 'pass 'em over there. They've got enough hot air to fill a gasometer.'

Children were arriving, asking what was going on and whether the Queen was coming. I told them about our visitor, and how he held the purse strings to the country's finances. 'He'll talk to your mums,' I said, 'and he might even talk to you. So tell him about the school garden...'

One of them soon spotted the stickers, and the children quickly realised the aides weren't sure who'd been given one and who hadn't. By hiding stickers under their coats they could keep going back, saying they hadn't had one. Ten minutes later, Year 5 looked like walking sticker banks.

Meanwhile, Mr Brown had arrived in his chauffeured motor, and was already shaking hands with a growing crowd of people. I admired his conversational skill, and he was completely unfazed by one of our parents helpfully suggesting that the prime minister was a fucking liar. Then it was time for the whistle, and the road show moved on.

In assembly, I asked the children what questions he'd asked. 'What's your best subject?' seemed the favourite. I trusted they'd all said 'gardening, but we don't have quite enough money to finish the school garden...'

Only Tommy had a longer conversation, but then, Tommy would. The main thrust of it seemed to consist of Gordon pointing out very firmly that, no, the party worker standing alongside him *wasn't* his girlfriend.

55

Foyez is wondering which end makes marks on the paper

Even though I'm a headteacher, I still do a fair amount of teaching, and my Monday afternoons are reserved for literacy with Year 6. We divide the children into ability groups and for several years I've had the pleasure of teaching those who enjoy literature and are, in many cases, becoming accomplished writers.

But not this year. I've set myself a challenging target and opted for the 'less able': the ones who struggle with reading and aren't that keen on picking up a pencil for anything, let alone creating sentences.

They're taken aback when they discover I'll be taking the class, realising they'll need to be inventive with their methods of work avoidance. They eye me cautiously as I appear in the doorway for the first lesson.

I give out nice new books and we make colourful covers. They like this bit very much.

Then comes the hard part. I explain that writing is actually great fun, that I love it to bits, and by the end of the year they'll be enjoying it just as much as me. They don't believe a word of this, and already their attention is drifting: Bo is dissecting his rubber, Jadie is ferreting through her tray, and Foyez is looking at his pencil as if wondering which end makes marks on the paper.

Abdul suddenly peers at me intently and his hand shoots into the air. He asks with genuine curiosity: 'Sir, why do your eyebrows go up and down when you talk?'

'Thank you very much, Abdul,' I reply. 'I wasn't aware that they did.' For the next half hour I concentrate on keeping my eyebrows still as I speak. It isn't easy.

I tell them we're going to write about things we know well, and I ask them to shut their eyes and cast their memories as far back as possible. Then I describe my own first day at school as an infant, remembering how my mother deposited me in the classroom and beat a hasty retreat, hoping I wouldn't notice. I did of course, and rushed out of the classroom into the playground, where she'd locked herself in the lavs, again hoping I wouldn't notice. The teacher peeled me from the toilet door like a bluebottle off a flypaper and dragged me, sobbing, back into the classroom.

The group enjoy this story, and we talk about everything we do to make everybody's first day at Comber Grove a happy one. I ask them to think about their own very first day at school and write about it. I say that I'll give them a few moments to put their thoughts together.

They chatter excitedly over 'do you remember?' anecdotes, and then gradually settle into silence. Darren, never one for writing, says he needs the toilet. 'Of course,' I say loudly for everyone's benefit, 'as soon as you've finished your writing.' Foiled, he gazes blankly at his page and says he can't think of anything. I explain that all writers experience that problem at times, but something will come into his mind soon. And eventually it does, because he doesn't fancy sitting bored stiff for the next half an hour.

By the end of the lesson they've written a reasonable amount. It's ragged, but laced with enthusiasm. They're eager to read aloud, and Abdul's story is riveting. He writes descriptively about his first teacher in Sierra Leone, who smelt badly and whose wife left him. 'So, guys,' he writes in his last sentence, 'if you want to keep your womun mak sure you use plenty of sope.' The group nods appreciatively.

As the whistle blows the following Monday, Jadie runs up to me and asks if we have literacy. 'Indeed we have,' I say. 'Yes!' she says, punching the air.

Who knows, by the end of the year my 'less able' group might be more able than they'd imagined.

56

Teachers need time and space to breathe

What have we come to? In a recent poll, a significant number of primary school teachers admitted they were now so used to cramming for SATS tests they simply wouldn't know what to teach if the tests were abolished.

I worry a lot about the disappearing art of teaching. People should teach if they can give children a real enthusiasm for learning; if they can inspire them, make them laugh, make them care about each other and give them a passionate interest in the world around them. In turn, children have an absolute right to expect their teachers to be stimulating, knowledgeable people, not boring automatons who are endlessly worrying about targets and handing out photocopied worksheets.

But rather than trust teachers to get on with the job, our leaders constantly try to crack nuts with sledgehammers. It's not that long ago since primary schools had a 'literacy hour' forced upon them. It came down like a lead balloon and was about as interesting.

Prescriptive, constricting, and costing a fortune, it did precious little to encourage children to become avid readers or writers. And just in case any teachers considered introducing it in anything but the prescribed manner, even the words they had to say were included in the pack.

When I started teaching in the sixties, the Plowden Report was transforming primary education. There were no SATS tests to worry about or cram children for, no complex and detailed lesson plans to be handed in every day for scrutiny by senior managers who've spent so much time out of the classroom they've forgotten what a child looks like.

Of course, I planned my lessons – in detail – and my plans fitted into the school's individual and carefully devised curriculum, but there was no one peering over my shoulder every two minutes to check I had ticked the appropriate boxes or accounted for every second of the day.

Teachers had time and space to breathe. They could organise the day in a way best suited to their children, and while some ran a fully integrated day, in my classroom the mornings tended to be skills-based and intensive, while the afternoons were used for a large variety of practical topics. At least you had the freedom to choose. And, importantly, the curriculum could be made really exciting, because there was an opportunity to spend a lot of time on a particular project if we wanted to.

I remember undertaking a topic on the cinema, after teaching several lessons to my Year 6 class about the influence of the media. We'd been concerned about the amount of litter in the school grounds, and since the school had a movie camera and a sound projector, we decided to make a short film about it.

The children produced story outlines, one was chosen, and a story-board designed. A creature arrives from Planet Tidy, is horrified to see children dropping litter, and uses its amazing powers to make the litter jump back on to the children who dropped it.

A simple idea, but making the 15-minute film involved three weeks of intensive work: acting, writing, directing, science, art, special effects, scripting, problem-solving. We also had to design and build a creature that could be animated convincingly. One morning, a parent stopped me as I was lining my class up at the start of the day. 'I don't know what you're doing,' she said, 'But my David can't wait to get to school these days. He loves it.'

Eventually, the film was finished and ready for its premiere. We advertised (lots to be learned here, too!), each class was shown the film, and a screening was also held for the parents. It was a great success, and other classes were encouraged to write reviews and articles, and to take up the theme of keeping the school tidy.

These days, I'm always delighted when I see capable young teachers finding inventive ways of tackling the national curriculum. Nevertheless, when I peer through my rose-tinted spectacles, I tend to think that children in the less prescriptive days often had the best of it.

57

If Conan Doyle were alive his detective would be called Ayomide

September, and all the children are settled happily in their new classes. I've almost forgotten the detective games they play at the end of the summer term, trying to find out which teacher will be taking which class the following year.

I learned how not to do it when I was a deputy head. The whole school would be brought into the hall on the Monday of the last week, and the head would name a teacher and call out the children who were going to be in his or her class.

I remember Margo Huggins punching the air and shouting 'Yes!' when she heard that she was to be with me, whereupon the head peered distastefully through her spectacles at Margo and said: 'I hardly think Mr Kent will want you in his class if you make silly noises, young lady.' Of course, I was secretly flattered that Margo was so keen to be in my class, but I also felt sympathy for the teacher who received only a faint but audible groan.

Which is why children at my school don't know their new classes until the last day of term, and they're told in their classrooms, not the hall. Nevertheless, the most inquisitive pupils ask well before the term ends.

At first, they slip a question to Secretary Sandra when they collect a piece of fruit or a plaster. 'Have you done the lists for next year, Miss?' they'll ask sweetly. 'Do you know what class I'll be in?' When

Sandra professes to know nothing, despite having compiled the lists weeks ago, the child changes tack. 'Then do you know what class my friend Gloria will be in, Miss? I won't tell anyone, honest.'

Eventually, they give up. But not Ayomide. If Conan Doyle were still writing, his detective would be called Ayomide, because Ayomide knows everything, and what he doesn't know he can find out. He often comes to my room asking if I have any jobs, and his eyes roam quickly over every piece of paper on my desk and noticeboards. This year, when a lot of children suddenly seemed to know which classes they'd be in, I remembered I'd left the new lists on Sandra's desk that morning... and she'd been visited by Ayomide just before playtime.

Counter-measures were called for. I wrote a hasty note, saying that we'd be joined in September by some new teachers, including Mr Wackford-Squeers, Mr Chips, and Miss Jean Brodie. I also pointed out that Sandra would be teaching Year 6 each day, once she'd counted the dinner money.

I summoned Ayomide and asked if he'd be kind enough to take the note to all the teachers, stressing that it was confidential and that on no account should he look at it. By playtime, children were asking which teachers were leaving to make room for the new ones, and this Mr Wicked-Squares sounded a bit posh, didn't he?

But it isn't just the children who are inquisitive. Parents want to know which teachers will be honoured with their offspring, too and as usual they had been ringing for the last couple of weeks to find out. Even so, I was totally unprepared for the visit from Mrs Andrews, a well-endowed mother, on the last Monday of term.

'Are you in the mood for a bribe?' she asked enticingly.

'Sorry,' I said. 'I'm as honest as the day I was born.'

'Oh go on,' she said. 'Tell me what class my Emily is going to be in and I'll give you a nibble on me baps.' I stepped back... and then realised she was referring to her bag of cheese rolls.

Now who said being a headteacher doesn't have its moments...

58

Grammar and spelling weren't considered important

Consider this snippet of a TV host recently congratulating a contestant on a talent show: 'That was fantastic! You were brilliant, just brilliant! What a fantastic voice!'

Contestant: 'It was fantastic. I've had such a fantastic time.'

Host: 'That's so fantastic.'

Or this conversation overheard in the playground at my school:

'Where did you went?

'Where did I went when?'

'That time. When you wasn't in school.'

'I weren't well.'

'I see your mum. Innit you've had a chicken's pox though?'

What is happening to our language? Forty years ago, a colleague walked into a shoe repairer and complained about a sign in the window that said, 'Shoes mended while U wait'. How could we teach children to use English well, he asked, if they were being subjected to signs like that?

How trivial it seems now. We can accept text messages peppered with shorthand such as 'IMHO' ('in my humble opinion') and 'FWIW' ('for what it's worth') because there is a reason for the brevity, but the poverty of language and standard of spelling and grammar in everyday life is truly worrying. The government seeks to address the problem with its literacy hours and language targeting, but we often seem to be swimming against the tide.

A free local newspaper which came through my door recently was riddled with errors. Banner headlines told us the new 'Naborhood Center' was progressing, train services were still 'appaling', and teachers had 'disipline' problems 'dispite' smaller classes. Page 2 contained no less than 18 obvious errors, and I could read no further. People who write in newspapers usually have a fondness for the correct use of language. Was I witnessing the birth of a worrying new journalistic standard?

Even supposedly serious publications are often full of mistakes. In newspapers, I've seen: 'Are you paying too much comission?'; 'Put our advise into practise'; and 'We're a fully independant company.'

These days, no one seems to have heard of colons or semi-colons, either; commas have taken their place and sentences are merely run into each other. The advertisement quoted above also said: 'Mortgage brokers receive fees, these are paid by the lender.'

So who's to blame? Well, we'd better start with the teachers. Many younger teachers were educated in the days when everything in literacy was subordinate to the 'creative flow'. Grammar, spelling and syntax weren't important; the main thing was to get the ideas on paper. Teachers were told not to put discouraging marks on their pupils' work because it might put them off writing forever. Looking back, it seems amazing that so-called 'educational experts' can have been so daft, but they certainly did some damage. One teacher at my school spelled 'vocabulary' and 'verbal' wrongly on every one of her school reports.

But parents must take some of the blame, too. Often, they are hardworking people who haven't got much time to spend with their children. They don't talk to them, let alone read a book with them or have a conversation, even though such basic activities are crucial in developing language skills. A child who has been given a literacy-rich start at home stands out, from nursery age onwards.

142

Teachers simply don't have time to extend children's language as much as they'd like, either. An awful lot now has to be crowded into the school day.

Nevertheless, although I sometimes look back through rose-tinted spectacles, it wasn't all perfect. I remember an education authority sending a directive to teachers stating its concern about 'litracy' standards. They withdrew it hours later, of course, very shame-faced.

Quite right too, FWIW, IMHO.

59

The firemen are bound to be thirsty

'You asked to see me, headmaster?'

'Ah, Daphne, come in. So how are we doing on the entertainment front?'

'As well as can be expected, headmaster, but you've set me quite a task.'

'I know, Daphne, I know. But the *Times Educational Supplement* said the Department for Education and Science spent £636,420 on entertainment last year.'

'What, educational fact-finding tours abroad? That sort of thing?'

'Oh no, that comes out of an entirely different pot. This is simply for entertaining visitors during the year at the DfES. Cucumber sandwiches, cups of tea, the odd bottle of Beaujolais...'

'That's an awful lot of money, headmaster.'

'It is, isn't it. Presumably they put a lot of cucumber in the sandwiches. Anyway, if they're spending that much, entertaining must be a crucial element of education. And we must follow their wisdom. How are things going?'

'Well, the inspector's still sitting in the staffroom.'

'And you're looking after him?'

'As you suggested, I pointed him in the direction of the sherry. He's smiling a lot. And he keeps falling off the chair. Oh, and I'm afraid there's no sherry left.'

'Jolly good. That's got rid of a few bob. Added bonus, too: he won't be going round the classrooms irritating everybody. Shame we haven't got an Ofsted inspection. We could have flattened the entire team. What about the governors' meeting tonight?'

'I bought some new crockery, headmaster. Bone china. Harrods' best. I bought some new teaspoons, too. Solid silver. And I could make them some snacks. Canapes, vol-au-vents, cheeses, a bit of smoked salmon...'

'Splendid! Get a catering team in to do it. It'll be more expensive. Got to entertain them properly, anyway. And what about all the other visitors we have? Educational psychologists, students, welfare officers, training lecturers....?'

'I've ordered Earl Grey, Jasmine, Assam, Darjeeling, and 15 varieties of coffee. But headmaster, don't you think...'

'Good, good, we're getting there. Give 'em all a hamper from Fortnum and Mason as well. Perhaps we could do something for the parents at next week's Open Evening? What about a barrel of real ale and a bucket of chicken nuggets? And sticky buns and a big bag of sweets for the children?'

'I'll make a note of it, headmaster. Now, I really must get on. The firemen will be here any minute to talk to Year 6.'

'I'd forgotten about the firemen! They're *bound* to be thirsty after taking Year 6. I get thirsty even thinking about taking Year 6. Better get in a dozen crates of lager, Daphne.'

'Is that a good idea? Health and safety...'

'Hmm. Probably not. They'll be spraying their hoses all over the place. Make it Lucozade and a couple of hot dogs each. Now then Daphne, tot that little lot up and tell me how we're doing.'

'It comes to, um, just over £900, headmaster.'

'Damn, is that all? How does the DfES do it? They've spent seven hundred times as much as us.'

'I wonder, headmaster... it's just an idea, of course... couldn't we go back to giving everybody the standard cup of tea, and then spend the money we save on the children? You know, musical instruments or something like that?'

'Good idea, Daphne, I never thought of that! Perhaps the DfES hasn't thought of it either. I'll give them a ring. It could start a new trend...'

60

Don't you lot have contingency plans?
How did we win the war?

We had to close the school on Wednesday, something I haven't had to do for 18 years. That was when the snow was so bad many teachers couldn't get to school, and our struggling boiler simply gave up and broke down.

This time it was a fuse. Not just any old fuse, mind, but a huge 160 amp job, encased in metal and as big as your fist. There was a nasty smell and an acrid whiff of smoke from the main electrical cupboard in the hall, and the lighting on the corridors suddenly died, plunging large areas of the school into darkness.

Classroom assistants searched the toilets, retrieving terrified infants who'd stumbled for the door. Premises officer Dave checked the contact breakers, while teachers poked their heads around doors demanding to know which twerp from Year 6 had switched the lights off.

The problem quickly escalated. Our cook hurried upstairs to tell me that her freezers were down and it wouldn't be that long before the supplies started thawing out. I had to make a quick decision. I didn't want to close the school, but if we couldn't feed the children we didn't really have much option.

After a hasty consultation, the cook decided she could do sandwiches and salad, and the teachers said they could manage one day in semi-darkness. I breathed a sigh of relief... until Dave told me the boilers had gone down too. There'd be no heating or hot water. Now there was no alternative; we would have to close.

It was too late to get a letter to the parents, so we rang the LEA for the name of a reliable electrician. One arrived quickly, and probed the fuse cupboard with a torch and a test meter. 'That's your problem!' he said triumphantly, pointing to a massive fuse.

'So can you change it?' I asked.

There was a sharp intake of breath. 'It's a very old one. Been there years. I reckon it'll take a good couple of days to find one of these. If we can even find one, that is. Frankly, I doubt it.'

He hurried off to track down what he thought we needed, and another electrician rang, saying that he'd done lots of work for the LEA and, whatever it was, he'd be with us in 10 minutes and guarantee to fix it within the hour. He tested the fuse the first man had isolated.

'Nothing wrong with that,' he said. 'There's a fault somewhere else.'

Half an hour later he found a tiny cupboard tucked away in a classroom and a second massive, ancient fuse. Another sharp intake of breath. 'Tough one, that. Might get it for Friday.'

Next morning, Dave stood by the gate, explaining why children couldn't come in to the school. Most parents, as usual, were very understanding. Mr Smith, as usual, wasn't.

'So what's all this about, then?'

'Sorry, we've no lighting, heating, hot water, or cooked meals.'

'Don't you lot have any contingency plans for emergencies?'

'Not for this, I'm afraid. It's a unique situation. We've never had this one before.'

'Well, it's fucking inconvenient. God only knows how we managed to win two world wars.'

He stalked off down the road, his wife trailing behind him and looking embarrassed. Neither of them work for a living, but the idea of simply looking after his three very lively children for an extra day must have been anathema.

Fortunately, the second electrician found a fuse by midday, the building was soon light and warm again, and the children were back the next day. On Friday, I received a call from a parent governor.

'Is school open again, then?' she asked. 'Nobody wrote and told us.'

I made a mental note to make a public announcement on the Ten O'Clock News if it ever happens again.

61

Children were scrabbling up the walls trying to get a view

The neighbourhood surrounding our school isn't known for its tranquillity, and we'd had a gangland shooting in the main road at the weekend. There was a murmur of gossip about it as the children filed into school on Monday morning, and then it seemed to be gradually forgotten.

Until Wednesday lunchtime, when a classroom assistant hurried up to me as I munched my meat and two veg.

'A bloke has just rushed into the corridor,' she said. 'Says he's being chased. Can you have a word with him?' Several children had overheard the helper and were peering outside as I approached the man. He was leaning against a cupboard, panting.

'I need help, mate,' he said. 'I'm a reporter and I went to interview the family of the bloke who was shot. I'm being chased by a gang of youths.'

I'd heard this kind of thing before. Years ago, a woman walked into the office, said she wanted to register her 15 children and then began to remove her clothes. Last year, a gentleman who told the children he was an inspector quietly removed three handbags from the staffroom and legged it over the wall. People aren't always what they seem.

I asked if he had any identification. He produced a laminated card with a faded photo and a title saying 'Press'. I wasn't convinced, but he seemed genuine enough. By this time, faces were staring through the hall doors with interest, and I suggested that we walk towards the gate, away from the children. He blanched.

'I'm not going out there, mate. They'll kill me. I need police protection.'

I said Dave, our premises officer, was in the playground, and he had a mobile, so we'd get him to phone the police immediately.

More children gathered as we came outside, and Dave summed up the situation in a flash. Within minutes, a police car and a police van roared up the road, sirens blasting. By now, children were scrabbling up the walls, hanging over the fences, or lying flat on the playground floor trying to get a view under the solid metal gates. I led the 'reporter' quickly outside, explained the situation to the boys in blue, and left them to deal with it. I never did find out whether he really was a newsman.

Persuading the children nothing much was happening was a bigger task.

Rumours shot around the playground and Daniel, never our best attender, ran up and asked if school would be closed tomorrow. It occurred to me that I should write and reassure the parents, but I quickly dismissed the idea. After all, nothing much had really happened.

The phone calls began at eight the following morning. Was it safe to come to school, asked Mrs Gray; Samantha had said three gunmen were holed up in the school yesterday and there were rumours one was still in the building.

Is it true the school will be closed for three days, asked Mrs Williams, only Daniel said some of the teachers had been trapped in the corridor and one had been attacked.

Why weren't we alerted about all this, demanded Annie's mum, who cries bully if somebody so much as brushes against her daughter.

Are you all right, asked a friendlier parent, only I heard you'd been attacked by a huge man who rushed into the corridor yesterday...

Within a day normal service had been resumed, but I had to smile when our local minister, one of our parents, came in to take an assembly at the end of the week.

'I hear you're a hero,' he said. 'I'm told you were chased round the playground by a man with a samurai sword, and you grappled him to the ground in seconds.'

Spider-man, eat your heart out.

62

He'd had a wonderful time with the train set

Getting in or out of our school is like trying to break into Fort Knox.

We've just had another three security cameras fitted and aimed at the various entrances. Steve McQueen might just be able to leap over the wall on his motorbike, but he'd still have to crack the combination code on the front door.

How things have changed in the past couple of decades. When I came to Comber Grove, anybody could walk in, and frequently did, although I don't recall any particular sense of danger.

And we had at least one burglary a year. I'd been at the school for two months when thieves broke through the nursery door and helped themselves to the school photograph money. Two weeks later a thief nipped into the kitchen, removed the cook's Christmas savings from her handbag and legged it over the wall. And I'd just formed a guitar group when two youths wandered in, grabbed the newest guitars and made off down the corridor. Fortunately I spotted them, chased them around the building and cornered them in a washroom. They dropped the guitars and fled. These days, I'd probably be whacked over the head with them.

Occasionally though, I have to admire the cheek of the dubious characters we come across. One afternoon, a teacher rushed into my office saying her new class computer had been removed. Did I know why, or where it was? I hadn't a clue. The door had been locked at lunchtime, and nobody had seen or heard anything. Until another member of staff shed light on what had happened. 'Oh God,' she said. 'A chap in a white coat asked me where Jaine's classroom was because he had to take her computer for repair. And I opened the door for him!'

We weren't certain how the thief knew where to look, but there's always a buzz of excitement among the children when a new piece of technology arrives, and unfortunately the excitement sometimes reaches into the shadier regions of the local community. These days, we tell the children that our new pieces of technology might be very exciting, but we don't want the whole neighbourhood knowing about them.

It's unusual to feel sorry for a thief, but I did feel sympathy for the one who broke in through the Nursery door – again – one weekend. When the teacher arrived on Monday, she found the train set and several constructional games carefully laid out on the carpet. Nothing was missing, and apart from the broken door nothing had been damaged. He'd obviously had a wonderful time playing with the toys and then gone home again. I could only assume creative play hadn't featured strongly in his formative years.

These days, with all our security features, and the premises officer's alsatian dog who'd have the trousers off a thief before he'd climbed two feet up the wall, break-ins are very rare.

But that doesn't mean we can drop our guard. Recently, technicians fitting new equipment couldn't finish by hometime, and a set of loud-speakers was left in the bottom corridor. By next morning, they'd disappeared. No problem, we could scan through the video tapes and spot the mum in the heavy coat who'd suddenly become very pregnant. Except that the camera pointing at the only escape route had decided to pack up that evening.

And yes, the security code on the main door is a great idea, but, children being what they are, they delight in spotting it when staff forget to cover the buttons with their hand. On average, Dave, the premises officer, changes it every fortnight, and since I have trouble remembering my own house number I usually forget it immediately.

Which is why I can often be spotted wandering around the building early in the morning, hoping that someone's arrived before me so that I can tap on their window and get them to let me in.

63

So you want to be a school governor?

Apparently it's becoming hard to recruit school governors.

I'm not surprised. I'm not even sure what makes people want to become governors. A little power, maybe? A political leg-up? Some spare time to offer and a heart full of good intentions?

Certainly, their workload and responsibilities are awesome. They hire and fire, oversee the curriculum, listen to complaints from parents, and tell the head how the school's money should be spent. Major decisions must be approved by them. And they must form themselves into committees to discuss and evaluate every aspect of school life.

Which is fine when a school is running like a well-oiled machine, but what happens when it isn't? Well, they can simply walk away. They're unpaid volunteers, after all. What an eccentric system it all seems. And occasionally this gives rise to eccentric people, because, like juries, governing bodies contain a fair cross-section of society.

Some, like Hilda, I've been delighted to see the back of. A religious fanatic with time on her hands, she spent a great deal of time examining the school's religious education policy in excruciating detail and visiting classrooms to make sure it was being adhered to. For several months she was accompanied by the newest addition to the family, and wasn't averse to popping an ample breast out for the baby, often while the teacher was in full flow. I've never seen children distracted so quickly.

Then there was Allun, an empty vessel who made a great deal of noise, but never seemed to be available when there was work to be done or a committee to be attended. I'd bet a year's salary there's at least one Allun on every school governing body in the country.

But for every pain in the neck there's always a deeply committed and enthusiastic soul, even though there can be a little naiveté about the realities of school life. Eleanor was a newly appointed parent governor who wasn't a great fan of our playground toilets. They may be Victorian, she said, but couldn't we put decent paper, in decent holders, on the cubicle walls, just like we have on the inside ones? Couldn't the children have soap, and paper towels? We explained that the playground helpers carried all these things in a bag, as we'd had lots of problems when they'd been put in the toilets. 'But the children are so well behaved here,' she persisted. 'Couldn't we try it again?' We did, and I waited with bated breath.

By Thursday, it looked as if it had been snowing. A visiting afterschool group had decided there was a lot of fun to be had from decorating the school garden with Tesco's best.

Then, on Friday, things took a turn for the worse in the shape of a large forehead lump, a swollen eye and a cut lip. Infants Billy, Rashid and Thomas had been playing 'Pirates of the Caribbean' (not a risk assessment in sight), using the paper towels to fashion pirates' hats and the little bars of soap as missiles.

Billy had dodged the missiles by hiding under a sink, but then cracked his head on it when he stood up. Following a further week of incidents, the governor agreed it might be best if we went back to the old system, whereby the materials were freely available from the duty helper's bag, but you had to ask first.

Nevertheless, I respect the enthusiasm of new governors, although this enthusiasm can sometimes be tempered by a rude awakening, as it was on the morning I was explaining the security system to our new deputy chairman. Looking up at the monitor, he watched a parent hover by the main gate for a few moments, and was then astonished to see her stuff the recently delivered staffroom milk under her coat and disappear rapidly down the street.

64

People like you often make very effective advisers and inspectors

Welcome to the seminar, everyone. My name's Grahame, nice to have you aboard. Please feel free to use all the hotel facilities, as the borough is paying. Now, you've joined the Group for Raising Academic Standards and Performance, or GRASP as we're known. I want to explain the building blocks that make us so successful. Let's start with a question. Who are we, and why are we here? Clarence?

'Um... educationally, this is a failed borough, and you're the private company that's been brought in to sort it all out.'

'Absolutely, Clarence. And how are we going to do that? Trevor?'

'Well, you'll need to get to know all the schools. I imagine you'd get out there and visit...'

'Whoa, let me stop you right there, Trevor. Visiting is not on our agenda for school improvement. No, our role is to advise.'

'But how can you advise if you don't understand your territory? If you want to add a conservatory to your house, don't you get the builder to look at the house first?'

'Nice analogy, Andrew, but inapplicable here, I'm afraid. You need to see the short-term view. One company has already been... well... asked to move on. We may not be here for very long. We need to maximise our potential in the shortest possible time. Take the shrewd option. Give out lots of advice...'

'And make a healthy profit?'

'Not a word I'm very fond of, David, but everybody has to eat.'

'Forgive me Grahame, but your advice to schools seems to consist of a set of questionnaires.'

'Not questionnaires, Simon. We refer to them as Points for Discussion. Our latest has 135 of them. Our people worked on it for weeks.'

'But how can busy headteachers possibly spend time poring over that?'

'Ah, well, that's the dilemma, isn't it? If they don't bother with it, we can say we're trying hard but the heads aren't interested. If they do bother with it, our people collate all the answers and then we organise a conference. This throws up a new set of discussion points.'

'And you send out another document?'

'You've got your eye on the ball, Simon. We're very proud of our discussion documents. You'll notice we've drawn in some important phrases.'

'You mean like 'committing fully to harnessing a range of energies that aspire to a culture of learning and excellence?'

'Nicely spotted, Dennis! Excellence is our keyword. We use it a lot. Achieving excellence. Aspiring to excellence. Excellence for all. That sort of thing. Carry on like that, Dennis, and you'll be promoted to head of school improvement. Yes, I know you are a failed teacher, but people like you often make very effective advisers and inspectors. You'd be surprised.'

'So what would this range of energies actually be, Grahame?'

'Who knows, Sharon. We'd need steering committees, twilight workshops and lots of dialogue with various interested parties to decide that. Now, I want you all to look at the flow diagrams in your notepacks. Incomes, outcomes, process and purpose. Oh, and lots of colour, of course.'

'The charts seem very difficult to understand...'

'Understanding is not a word we recognise, William. The point is, they look impressive. We send out packs like these to all the schools and it creates the impression that we're moving the borough forwards. Driving up standards. Striving for excellence. You see, there's that word again. Now then, what did I give you to read last week?

'*Target Setting for Target Setters*, Grahame.'

'Thank you, Alison. An excellent work, although this week's is even more important. It's called '*The Emperor's New Clothes...*'